The Tragi-Comedy of Pen Browning

The Tragi-Comedy of Pen Browning

(1849-1912)

by

MAISIE WARD

With an Introduction by

ROBERT COLES, M.D.

Sheed and Ward, Inc.
and
The Browning Institute, Inc.

Copyright © 1972 by Maisie Ward. All rights reserved.

Introduction Copyright © 1972 by Robert Coles. All rights reserved.

Library of Congress Catalog Card Number: 72-1865
ISBN: 8362-0494-8

Sheed & Ward, Inc., 64 University Place, New York, N. Y. 10003
Sheed & Ward, Ltd., 33 Maiden Lane, London, W. C. 2E
The Browning Institute, Inc., Box 2983, New York, N.Y. 10017

Published 1972
Printed in the United States of America

CONTENTS

Illustrations	vii
Foreword	ix
Introduction by Robert Coles, M.D.	xi
Chapter 1: Unexpected Baby	1
Chapter 2: Small Boy	13
Chapter 3: The Adolescent	37
Chapter 4: Painting and Sculpture	63
Chapter 5: Marriage	72
Chapter 6: Doing His Own Thing	121
Chapter 7: As Pen is Still Remembered	135
Appendices	151
Selected Bibliography	159
Index	161

ILLUSTRATIONS

	Page
Pen's Christening Robe	
Courtesy of The Browning Society of London	73
Pen Browning, circa 1851. Pencil sketch by Euphrasia Fanny Haworth. Courtesy of Wellesley College	73
Robert Browning, 1853. Pencil sketch by Pen Browning. Courtesy of the Trustees of The British Museum	74
Casa Guidi, circa 1915 Courtesy of Fedele Centaro	74
Pen Browning, 1858 Courtesy of Wellesley College	75
Pen Browning on Horseback, 1859. Oil by Hamilton Wild. Courtesy of Wellesley College	76
Pen Browning with his mother, Rome, 1860 Courtesy of Wellesley College	77
Pen Browning, Paris, 1862 Courtesy of Philip Kelley	78
Pen Browning, circa 1864. Photograph by Mrs. Cameron. Courtesy of Wellesley College	79
Pen Browning with his father, circa 1869 Courtesy of Wellesley College	80
Pen with the Millais family in Scotland, circa 1873 Courtesy of Elaine Baly	81
"The Artist at Work." Oil by J. Heyermans, circa 1874. Courtesy of Wellesley College	82
Pen's Exhibition Medals Courtesy of Wellesley College	83
"Still-life Study." Water-color by Pen Browning. Courtesy of Wellesley College	84
"Vespers." Oil by Pen Browning. Courtesy Misses Ruth and Vera Edminson	84

Page

"The Moonrise." Oil by Pen Browning.
   Courtesy of Wellesley College 85
"The Cobbler." Oil by Pen Browning.
   Courtesy of Wellesley College 86
"A Woman at her Devotions." Oil by Pen Browning.
   Courtesy of Wellesley College 87
"Pompilia." Bust by Pen Browning.
   Courtesy of Wellesley College 88
"Hope." Bust by Pen Browning.
   Courtesy of Elaine Baly 89
"Dryope." Statue by Pen Browning.
   Courtesy of Elaine Baly 90
"Nude Study." Oil by Pen Browning.
   Courtesy of Yaddo........................... 91
"Dinant on the Meuse." Oil by Pen Browning.
   Courtesy of Wellesley College 92
"The Gleaner." Oil by Pen Browning.
   Courtesy of Elaine Baly 93
"Bust of Robert Browning." Marble by Pen Browning.
   Courtesy of Balliol College 94
"Portrait of Robert Browning." Oil by Pen Browning.
   Courtesy of Yaddo 95
Fannie Coddington, 1872
   Courtesy of Elaine Baly 96
Pen Browning, circa 1885. Photographs by W. H. Grove.
   Courtesy of Elaine Baly 97
Wedding Photograph, October 4th, 1887
   Courtesy of Elaine Baly 98
Pen and Fannie, circa 1887
   Courtesy of Elaine Baly 99
Palazzo Rezzonico, 1890. Interior of a state-room.
   Courtesy of Wellesley College 100
Palazzo Rezzonico, 1890. Interior of private drawing-room.
   Courtesy of Wellesley College 101
Caricature of Pen Browning. Ink drawing, attributed to
   Alfred Barrett. Courtesy of Edward R. Moulton-Barrett . 102
Street Scene at Asolo
   Courtesy of Mrs. Norman Walker 102
Pen with his Aunt Sarianna, 1895
   Courtesy of Philip Kelley 103
Pen's Grave at Asolo, July 8th, 1913
   Courtesy of Elaine Baly....................... 104

FOREWORD

This little book came into being through the request of Philip Kelley that I write an Introduction for a collection of Browning's letters to his son. As with all Browning's prose writings there is a pedestrian quality about these letters curiously troubling to an admirer of his poetry. And it is noteworthy that, while poems abound not only to his wife but on the wife-husband relationship, he never wrote one to or about the son he adored and of whose upbringing he and an equally adoring mother made such a mess. As it happened, the publication of the letters had to be delayed, and my "Introduction" had grown to be a book, large enough to need an Introduction of its own, which Dr. Robert Coles has so very ably provided.

That Pen Browning did eventually escape, did become a person in his own right, worth more than the few lines assigned to him by most of the poet's biographers, emerges I hope from what I may call in words once much used, now long out of date, "this unvarnished tale." There is no moral in it save for parents who happen to be geniuses.

My best thanks go to Mrs. Veva Wood, research consultant of the Armstrong Browning Library at Baylor University; to Dr. Jack W. Herring, its director; to

Mrs. Norman Walker (Hélène Sullivan) and Mrs. John Beach for their recollections of Asolo; to Freya Stark and Messrs. John Murray for permission to quote her description of that small city; to Miss Myrtle Moulton-Barrett, Edward R. Moulton-Barrett, Esq., Col. Ronald A. Moulton-Barrett, and Dr. Lola Szladits of the Berg Collection of the New York Public Library, for granting me access to Barrett family papers; to Mrs. Violet M. Altham for supplying me with quotes from Surtees' diary; to Lady Berwick and Lady Mander for providing me rare source material and notes; to Messrs. John Murray for Browning copyright permissions; and above all to Philip Kelley for his unstinting help and sleuth-like power of discovery to which I owe so much information.

Maisie Ward

April 1972 *New York*

INTRODUCTION

Robert Coles, M.D.

At one point, as Maisie Ward valiantly tries to comprehend the relationship between the Brownings and their beloved son, she reminds us that "child psychiatry was an unknown science in those days"—meaning, all through the nineteenth century and the first years of this century. I am not at all sure that any one of today's various "experts," who claim to know so very much about children, can be of any real help to the author or readers of this book; in fact, I wonder whether the Brownings would have felt the need to avail themselves of those "experts," had they been available in England or Italy over a hundred years ago. Even more to the point, I am not so sure that the Brownings, all *three* of them, would have emerged any the better, had there been child psychiatrists like me in Rome, Siena, or London and had Mr. and Mrs. Browning been willing to take themselves and their growing child Pen for one or more "consultations."

I hesitate to start an introduction on such a skeptical note; I am in a sense undercutting my own credentials before I venture upon a particular "interpretation" of that extraordinary household Maisie Ward has sketched for us. Still, these days psychiatrists have much too much say in far too many matters, and are given an authority (as secular priests of sorts) that does not always serve them well—not to mention their uncritical (and often enough desperate) admirers. Nor is it fair to blame only what one hears described as the "lay public" for such a state of affairs. All one need do is go through the so-called psychiatric "literature" to understand why any number of people (hopefully their number is growing) feel moved to smile or frown, if not scream in indignation, because of this or that article, monograph, book. And God save the writers studied—it can be a scandal, what happens to their novels and plays and poems, the characters they have constructed out of their mind's sensibility, the ideas and passions, the subtleties of temperament, the nuances of social life, the ironies and ambiguities and contradictions and inconsistencies that reveal themselves so constantly in the course of our lives. I have in mind those gross simplifications that, in this instance, would have Elizabeth Barrett Browning an "over-protective" mother, among many other "bad" (here substitute "neurotic") things, and Robert Browning a "passive" or overly "dependent" father.

I dislike going even this far—making mention of the way some of us in this psychological-minded age handle (and devour) the lives of particular men and women and children. But I had better go even further, and as quickly as possible set down for the reader one train of thought I sadly know all too well—so that I can then show what is inadequate about any exceedingly influential contemporary manner of looking at people and their behavior. The story goes something like this: Pen was the only child of relatively old parents, who doted on him, paid him far too much attention, and not only spoiled him but set up in him certain unconscious resentments that are less easily discerned than his various loyalties, attachments or involvements, whether with people or ideas or projects. The result was a life propelled by powerful energies never acknowledged; and if to a certain extent that is how we all live, many of us (psychiatrists would argue) have not been so watched over, so indulged, so held up in virtual awe—hence we have no cause to feel as bitter and angry and fiercely defiant and self-pitying and self-defeating as Pen did, unknown to himself, of course.

I don't like that kind of schematic and persistently negative view of Pen's childhood. I don't like the overly theoretical literature of child psychology and psychiatry that passes itself off as "science," yet offers all of us, in one way or another troubled and confused, a new set of moralistic pieties. Still, one has to take wisdom, or at the very least, a bit of help, where one can get it—and I do think someone who does the kind of clinical work I do ought to ask the reader to stop and wonder about the lifelong burden created by over-zealous parents, too insistently preoccupied with a child.

As I went through Maisie Ward's manuscript I first was struck by the joy Pen inspired in not only the Brownings, but their staff, their friends and relatives, and even their correspondents, who apparently over and over again read those letters, all taken up with the child's everyday life, his words, his comings and goings, his efforts to assert himself or his moments of hesitation. Now, one might suppose that a child who by his very arrival caused so much happiness would himself be, in the main, happy—and continue to be so later on in life. What is more (since we live in an age filled with talk of "sibling rivalry") we have to remember that young Pen had no competitors, and just as important, his parents were not devoted to him because they had fallen away from each other. One can feel the great love those two poets (and extraordinary human beings) felt for each other in so much of what they wrote, and was written about them. Nor is it likely that their boy had any bad luck so far as genes go. Most geniuses are not born but made (I believe), but neither do geniuses defy certain biological laws. The Brownings were neither retarded nor dull-average in intelligence. They were easily able to offer both themselves and the world a healthy, well-developed child, who showed every evidence at ages one, two, three (and on and on) of being thoroughly well endowed with native intelligence and in addition a good, strong body.

Why, then, the cumulative sense of sadness that at least this reader felt as he read about Pen? I mean sadness for the child Pen, let alone the grown man we end up *also* feeling a little troubled by, if not pity for. Is it that we want Pen to follow his parents, become a *third* Browning of the kind school-children read, then as college students meet up with again—and finally pore over when and if they become scholars? Was the child, and afterwards the man, rather "disturbed"—something we sense, even if we can't quite put our fingers on exactly what was wrong? Do we, quite simply, take annoyance at the spectacle of a child being so flagrantly (wantonly, I fear) spoiled—and does it offend our present-day psychological sensibilities (successors to, but not

Introduction | xv

wholly unlike, both Puritan and Victorian sensibilities) that the grown man Pen should vacillate so, never quite commit himself to a way of life, a job, a wife? I suppose we are disappointed somewhat with the older Pen, and maybe we do recognize that something in him went awry—even if (hopefully) we do not want to saddle him with all those grim psychiatric labels that can be misleading and even at times insulting, though upon occasion clarifying.

I fear, however, that something else gets in our way as we read about Pen, and I again have to be evasive as I begin to describe what I have in mind—for the simple reason that both Browning parents were equally evasive about the same thing as was their son all through his life. Here was a child, after all, about whom practically nothing bad or complaining was said for years and years —by a mother and father who were thoroughly sensitive, perceptive and psychologically astute. (If they lived before our kind of psychological sophistication arrived on the scene, then maybe they were both lucky and all the more astute, because less encumbered with jargon and that mixture of self-consciousness and self-importance that our social sciences often bequeath to those who pursue them.) I know that parents don't like to complain about their children, find fault with them, or advertise their difficulties in letters or by the spoken word. I know that there is a long tradition of sentiment that protects babies and even older children from sharp-eyed, gloomy, skeptical observers, who are always on the lookout for what *doesn't* work, what is wrong behind all the pleasant and appealing faces of children. Nevertheless one wonders whether young Pen was *ever* really disciplined, and if so, by whom. And I suspect that some of the hysteria his mother conveys as she virtually sings the child's praises has to do with her own struggle to push out of mind the darker side of childhood—*anyone's* childhood, however kind and thoughtful and considerate and understanding (or psychologically sophisticated) be the parents. What is more, if I were asked to guess at what went "wrong" with Pen as he grew up (I suppose something goes "wrong" with each of us, inasmuch as rarely do we measure up as adults to *all* the possibilities we demonstrate as children), I would have to say that for Pen throughout his life the issue of self-restraint was especially important, and never resolved.

When a child is given just about everything his or her heart craves at this or that moment, something is thereby both learned and not learned: desire is followed by satisfaction with impressive regularity, and so there is no need to hold on and wait and maybe experience a little hardship, sweat a little, persist in the fact of one or another complex and somewhat frustrating obstacle—because it is unheard of to meet them, those obstacles that prepare so many of us for life's inevitably troublesome moments. Put differently, Pen as a baby and child lived in a world whose exhilarating joy was purchased at a very definite price: the young prince, and he was indeed that in many respects, was not prepared to deal with the confinements, rigidities, and restrictions that the world places upon most people. No wonder, then, that he had trouble in college, and never really settled into the long haul of a conventional career. And it must have been especially hard for such a young man to face all of a sudden the rigors of a strict classical education—accompanied by the demands of a social life that was not meant to be fun but rather reflect the stern, self-justifying ethic of England's ruling classes and those who felt the need to follow their lead. Given so much, disciplined so little, Pen now had to submit, submit, submit—to demanding teachers, to a difficult course of study, to the arbitrary but carefully-regulated impositions of an intensely class-conscious society. Even artists and writers have to suffer in the face of, and systematically come to terms with, various conventions and orthodoxies—such as the arbitrariness of their particular guilds, not to mention those inner or psychological rules and edicts which can cramp the mind hard, but also evoke in it spirited resistance. Hopefully the result of such tension is a compromise which we call "art"—the product, that is, of a person's fight to express himself or herself within the confines of a particular craft or art-form, and do so in a manner that both frees the reader or viewer or listener but also ties him or her to a given tradition, however challenged by the artist.

Of course, Pen was not brought up to be a wild man, or a confidence-man who has been taught nothing about the ethical restraints we all require of ourselves and others around us. Obviously the child was disciplined, told no as well as yes, frowned upon as well as cheered and praised extravagantly. The question is: how much, with what consistency, and yes, with what devotion, for after all discipline is also an art, requires the same care and good judgment and sense of balance that a poet or composer or sculptor tries to mobilize. And speaking of "balance," those who describe children as *only* full of love and joy and spontaneity and the desire to learn and "express" themselves are ever so often not those who must spend the long, long hours that "bringing up" a child requires: hours spent coming to terms with the darker, more impulsive side of childhood; hours spent stopping the child, telling the child no, keeping the child from going here (lest he or she be immediately killed) or there (lest there be trouble or danger or disappointment or pain); and yes, hours spent teaching the child that anyone's willfulness or "spontaneity" has to be accommodated to the fact that millions and millions of us share space and time on this planet, hence are at one another's mercy in more ways than we often think about—no doubt because, thank God, we have indeed learned some minimum amount of self-control.

I am sorry if in this modern, proudly-sophisticated age I come forth with the old Puritan notion that "self-control" is very important; yet I do, in fact I *must*, and not because pieties are in order, but because anyone who has worked with troubled children (let alone brought up reasonably "normal" and "happy" ones) cannot for long escape noticing how much a growing child needs all that "self-control" literally implies: a sense of self and a sense of control over oneself. And it is in precisely this respect that little Pen Browning may well have suffered: his parents loved him so very much that they never for a minute could really think of him as living his own life, growing up to become someone other than their child—someone with control over his own destiny. If Elizabeth Barrett Browning was taken away when Pen was not yet fully grown, Robert Browning lived on, an exceedingly concerned and devoted father, sadder than he could perhaps bear to acknowledge, bereft in a final way, it seems—except for the boy whose life offered a reason to persist, a connection with what otherwise seemed irretrievable, and except perhaps for those moments and longer when the mind flexes itself and through reveries and daydreams (and nightmares) fashions a semblance of the past. So, the boy probably had to fight harder than most to become a man, and may well have remained more a child than most of us do all his life—though by no means do I want to turn the man into a nothing, a case history of sorts, a bundle of neuroses such as psychiatrists all too often dwell upon in such a way that they see little else, and manage to miss rather a lot.

Maisie Ward gives us a lively and well-rounded account of Pen Browning, even if necessarily an incomplete account, and one inevitably limited by time's ability to erase memories—and further hindered by a certain elusiveness or inscrutability in the "subject" himself. Pen had his faults but he was obviously a man of talent and imagination. He reached out to people and in turn obtained from them affection and upon occasion sustained friendship. (In this regard I am much inclined to accept Mabel Dodge Luhan's account, in which the man's over-all integrity and discretion come across—and in addition, his impressive willingness to turn the other cheek in the face of gossip, insults and slander. Maybe it is only a much-loved child who later on can ignore or be puzzled by such provocations.) Pen could also be energetic, resourceful, a shrewd observer, a competent and upon occasion inspired artist. He was no isolated, paralyzed man; if he had what we today call his "problems," he repeatedly sent off sparks of warmth and humor—nor was intelligent activity beyond his reach.

But he foundered, and finally one does begin to feel sorry for him as this biographical sketch draws to a close: his marriage was unsuccessful; his work never became fully realized; he loved and was loved (as a man, never mind as a child) but he seems to have been a lonely man, and there are moments when one even feels like calling him pitiable—and pity may stand as an ultimate low in the ladder of emotions that people direct at one another. I have no use for those who *explain* lives, wrap them up tidily with one or another formulation, but again, I can't help feeling that at least one important issue in Pen's life, one persisting, unyielding, and in the end, unsurmountable issue may be called his struggle for discipline: as a child he seems to have had not very much of it; and as a man he may well have felt at loose ends, unable to pull himself together and in fact *be*—be himself in a quiet, unassuming way that is not to be confused with the showy, endlessly self-conscious, proudly psychological and "existential" postures we in this century have adopted or found ourselves compelled to sanction.

Before I stop and let the reader go on to Maisie Ward's observations, I would like to make one more conjecture, and it is that and that alone, because I will be speaking of what *might* have been—if. If only Pen and his wife had been able to have a child, and especially, have a son —then I rather suspect the couple would have stayed together, and maybe Pen would even have found himself driven as an artist in ways he never actually could be in the course of the life he did live. Rather obviously his wife was in love with more than Pen; she loved the Brownings, loved their poetry, their intellectual and social prominence, their achievements. No doubt she, too, would have doted on a Browning infant, on *another* possible poet, on yet one more chance to make Robert and Elizabeth immortal in flesh as well as spirit. But for her husband I believe a child would have meant something else: an opportunity to assert himself, at last, as a father rather than a man who otherwise seemed unable to shake off being the dearly cherished personification of the love two famous poets had for one another. And when a man starts being a father in earnest, his larger life can change: he can put aside, "solve" in an apparent flash, so very much that has bogged him down, distracted or enervated him; he can look to the future, his own as well as his child's, and feel driven now to provide, build up, consolidate—rather than live out the past again and again. A son might have enabled Pen to stop being *the* son—and though I am sure Pen's wife would have paid such a child no less attention than Pen himself received as a baby, I would also be willing to hazard the guess that Pen as a father would have been less desperate than either of his parents were.

One says such things hopefully, not to exude professional authority, but as a reader's response to a particular person's rather interesting and unusual life, as portrayed in these pages. The longer I live, the more I try to do my work as a psychiatrist, the less impressed I am by all those psychological theories that try to tell us what causes what, what (inevitably it is said) leads to this, or precludes (by definition) that. Lives do indeed move along in response to various psychological urges ("drives") and necessities; but at every moment in our lives we are open to new possibilities, and are capable of turning in surprising directions. Accidents, unexpected incidents, fateful encounters—all of those developments and much else that is mysterious or elusive or hard to pin down in words go to make up what in the end (and only then) we who survive a particular person get to call his or her "life."

If as we read this account of Pen's life he seems at the end still very much in the grips of the unusual and fascinating (and at times unsettling) childhood that Maisie Ward evokes for us, then we are obliged to remind ourselves that it didn't have to happen like that; and what is more, in certain respects the grown Pen did indeed come forth as his very own person—so it wasn't *all* like that, anyway.

The Tragi-Comedy of Pen Browning

Chapter One

UNEXPECTED BABY

That she could give birth to a baby came as a surprise to Elizabeth Barrett Browning. After Browning had persuaded her to break away and they had been quietly married in London, they made their first home at Pisa. After some six months Elizabeth, one day not feeling very well, consulted a doctor who found her to be over five months pregnant. He could, he said, have saved her from a miscarriage had he been summoned sooner. Elizabeth wrote to her sisters furious over her own stupidity and one can only marvel that neither she nor Browning, nor her very intelligent maid Wilson had guessed what was happening. Elizabeth had, like many women, especially perhaps those who marry late, a tendency to miscarry and on either side of her first-born's birth came crises, one of them involving a loss of blood so great as to alarm both doctor and husband. So nervous had Robert become that Elizabeth wrote to Mrs. Jameson during this successful pregnancy: "He wished to heaven that the living creature would exhale and disappear in some mystical way without doing me any harm."

The Tragi-Comedy of Pen Browning

The child once safely delivered, the father's attitude became very different. At nine days old his son showed in Browning's eyes "indubitable signs" of being the "Coming man" hailed by Disraeli—"being blessed already with exalted genius, which nobody can give or take away." Victorian-wise he cut off little tufts of hair, sending them to Elizabeth's sisters, and his own mother, who was too near death even to understand the joyful news.

Her death cast for a while a shadow over the son's joy in being a father. But the joy persisted and grew as the little creature developed. Elizabeth admits to parental passion in herself and Robert: they longed and hoped for another baby, but Elizabeth persisted in miscarrying. Pen was in the event the one, the cherished, the over-cherished, child of a middle-aged mother and a father, who though younger than she by six years, was already thirty-six.

Before he was many months old the chronicle had begun which would continue for the rest of Elizabeth's life of the doings and very soon the sayings of Robert Wiedeman Barrett Browning—for so this little morsel of humanity (born in Casa Guidi at Florence on March 9th, 1849)* was christened. But almost as soon as he began to talk he named himself Penini, which gradually became Pen—and Pen Browning he remained.

There has seldom, I imagine, been so clinically detailed and exact an account of a childhood as Elizabeth gave to her sisters of this cherished offspring of hers. At not

---

*His certificate of birth and baptism is dated June 28th, 1849.

quite four months old her maid Wilson expected him "to get down and walk away ... if you put out your two fingers the child will seize them in his fists and drag himself up—would stand if allowed." Moreover "he understands everything: he plays with Flush's ears and talks to him."

Flush was Elizabeth's beloved dog, gift of Miss Mitford. His barking had had to be smothered as his mistress crept away from her father's house, where life-long imprisonment would have been the alternative to the happy marriage and a child whom others besides his parents felt to be unusual and remarkable.

Strangely enough Elizabeth interrupts her chronicle to reproach Arabel Barrett, the much-loved sister to whom she was writing, for "walking through alleys in Westminster and joining in crowded associations on hot evenings," in the interests of what were called her "ragged schools." But Arabel was helping to still that "Cry of the Children" which Elizabeth herself had once heard so clearly. Children taken from street or factory were given in these schools elementary instruction and helped towards better lives than their circumstances promised. For in the first half and more of the nineteenth century, factories were multiplying all over England, coal was being mined, and in mines and factories alike child labour had become an important element. It is startling to realize how long it was before anything was done for the protection of these children—even a bill to limit their work to *twelve* hours daily being hotly contested. And the parents were so badly paid that we find them driving the children to their toil for the sake of the miserable shilling or two added to their own scanty wage. Elizabeth Barrett had written:

> "For oh," say the children, "we are weary,
>   And we cannot run or leap—
> If we cared for any meadows, it were merely
>   To drop down in them to sleep. ...
> For, all day, we drag our burden tiring,
>   Through the coal-dark, underground—
> Or, all day, we drive the wheels of iron
>   In the factories, round and round."

Now she could think of nothing but this one most blessed babe—and when she does break off again it is to grow indignant over the shocking English habit of putting their children into cold water. The children always scream and Italian parents have no such barbarous ways of hardening them. In England, anyhow, this was a barbarous period in its treatment of the young—rich as well as poor.

By the time Pen's first birthday arrived, Elizabeth wrote recovering from one of her many miscarriages and fearing they could not get to England that year, "It won't quite do, to beg our way, with Baby playing on the tamburine [sic], though he plays it beautifully to be sure ... holding it up with one hand and playing it with the other. ... I think I told you that when he was eleven months old he stood without touching anything? However he crawls too well to care to walk."

Pen's first birthday had not been kept joyfully, being so near the anniversary of his grandmother's death—yet as well as a friend's gift of a white wooden horse ("he screamed with delight") they had given him a dog that barked and a cat that squeaked. Already he was "boy-like in all his ways" excepting his delight in being kissed and petted; "Passionate the child is certainly ... sullen and obstinate he never is ... with tears on his cheeks they dimple all over with joy again." By July he is walking, though "staggering like a drunken fairy" and still preferring to crawl.

They had serious trouble at first over the question of his food—for the doctor was firm that Elizabeth, despite having plenty of milk, must not nurse him. She had abandoned throughout her pregnancy the drugs prescribed originally by her English doctor, but probably he feared the latent tuberculosis which as far as can be guessed was at the root of her ill-health. Anyhow after frantic efforts a wet-nurse had been found, an Italian peasant who startled Wilson, the maid who had accompanied Elizabeth in her flight from her father's house, by liking to take off her shoes and stockings and run up and down the terrace. She was gay, healthy and good-natured, and for many months Pen was nourished whenever he liked from her bountiful supply of milk.

It was the oddest mixture at one year old—from hanging on the nurse's breast to sitting on his father's knees imitating his playing of the piano. Soon he was holding a pencil at exactly the angle he had observed and "writing" with an obvious satisfaction in his own achievement. Robert would set an empty inkstand beside him into which he dipped the pencil; carefully arranged in his father's attitude one leg over the other, he would spread open a book or unfold and spread out a letter which he would pretend to read: "Ah, ah, ba, ba, Papa." He would blow the fire with the bellows, dust the room, comb his hair. No wonder she claims he was "an accomplished baby" at sixteen months old.

Robert's letters of this period are rare but in July 1850 it was he who wrote to Arabel of "our boy (for he is clearly past babyhood) . . . strong as a colt," ordering them all about. If they do not obey the signals, for though he *can* talk he chooses rather to pull and push, nod or give other "inarticulate signs" of his wishes, "he stamps and wrings his hands that the world should be going so wrong."

Elizabeth had had yet another miscarriage and Pen a slight sunstroke—so slight as to be called more accurately a "suntap"—but both being better and Florence overhot, they moved near Siena, to a house with fruit-filled garden, which fruit Pen was bent on devouring. First he would point to it admiringly, then strike his breast with an "insinuating smile" to indicate his own cravings and then—if he was not forthwith supplied "a burst of grief" would follow. Distractions could be used—the pigeons, the chickens, the pig whose snout he liked to pat. But his temper was at this stage becoming a real problem and friends were urging upon his parents the well-known Victorian remedy mention of which some years later Elizabeth would furiously excise from children's books sent from England for Pen. In *Peep of Day* and *Line upon Line* she found statements that "only a Unitarian could accept." But above all she objected to the assertion "God has told fathers to beat their children to keep them from hell," which she called "a tender adaptation of scripture." Fire and brimstone, bodies burning forever, are "complacently dwelt upon." One can see today in the Armstrong Browning Library at Baylor University these "little books" in which, with astonishing skill, Elizabeth had substituted her own ideas for the offending passages before letting Pen read them.

At this date even he was not a reader, but Elizabeth noted a few months after the advice to whip was given that had they followed it the subsidence of Pen's infant passions would have been attributed to its salutary effect. Without their having done so, Pen had now become "miraculously good."

But was the stimulation too great? Wilson would say at times that it was—that he should be kept in the nursery like other children. He was indeed so excitable, Elizabeth admits, that Robert and she had asked one another whether he was going mad. However she put aside these fears with the remark that they wanted him happy and joyous and he was certainly both. But the splendid toys which he was already allowed to choose for himself at the shop brought on a state of excitement in which "it was frightful to see him."

Then too there were the frequent changes, the constant travelling. He was only just two when the first journey to England was made and, "sensitive to beauty," he was overwhelmed when they reached Venice and he was carried in Wilson's arms from the gondola to St. Mark's. He should have been exhausted from the journey, but more alive than any grown-up in the party, "he threw up his little hands with a shriek of joy" and further showed his delight by kissing Wilson. Then came "the Dogana del Mare with the great golden ball at the summit" and "he threw his hands out east and west and clasped them together crying 'O mama—O papa.' "

"Due" meant for Pen a large number, and, as they passed church after church, he cried "due, due" in a continuous chant. For he was at this age an intensely religious child. His own prayers were chiefly the regular

"God bless"—for parents, Wilson, his "balia" (the wet-nurse) and the dog Flush. But he would chant like the priests he had listened to, he talked of the "holy pigeons" that surrounded St. Mark's, he would light a candle as an accompaniment to his mother's prayers, "he stands opposite to me holding it and chanting at the top of his voice. When I get up he makes two curtsies . . . and taking one of my fingers prepares to go on in with me to the breakfast room." They found him one day taking the sacrament from her small medicine glass. Anglican and Catholic worship both figured in his spiritual exercises.

Elizabeth's own religion was profound but she had an intense hatred of sectarianism and she asks Arabel if she, as a good churchwoman, is shocked at their thinking it quite unnecessary to check Pen in his enthusiasm (one of the rare words that has grown richer instead of poorer in meaning) by warning him against Romanism. She knew English children in Italy who had been so taught that they saw nothing but evil in the religion that surrounded them. But Pen she felt could get nothing but good from the glorious singing, the intensely religious atmosphere. She was glad he liked priests almost as much as soldiers (they gave him sugar plums!). Sundays he would probably go with father and mother to a church of their choice, but Wilson was welcome and he eager to visit any Catholic churches they passed at any time, to look and listen—and to pray.

At Venice began a struggle between Elizabeth and Robert in which the woman was almost bound to gain the upper hand—especially at a time when children's garments were mostly made at home. Robert wanted to indicate by his clothes that Pen was a boy, not a girl. With his long golden curls and elegant dresses (copiously described in the letters) and even his feathered hat, he was, said Elizabeth, as yet of neither sex, only "a small angel travestied." And though she tells Arabel that Robert had had "the upper hand" in their dispute, all the descriptions indicate what outside evidence confirms, that Pen continued to be dressed in a picturesque and unusual style, which if not quite feminine was certainly not masculine. Photos show other children of the period dressed similarly and one feels Robert may have been oversensitive on the point. Yet as time went on Pen's clothes did become an obsession with his mother—an obsession not too healthy for any child, especially a boy. Embroidered trousers and exquisite blouses with lacy frills kept pace with his growth but not with any consideration of his age. Despite his entreaties as he grew older, his mother would not let him change from soft, polished leather shoes even when riding. So much did all this matter to her that once when a trunk was lost containing the manuscript of *Aurora Leigh* she was far more concerned about its other contents—Pen's elaborate wardrobe.*

They travelled on, pausing at Lucerne, where Elizabeth, almost dropping on the stairs from exhaustion, encountered a son who refused to go to bed any earlier than Papa and Mama and the horses. But in another letter written on arrival in Paris, Elizabeth again mentions Wilson's fears that Pen's high spirits mask the fact that he is overtired and overstrained. In a parenthesis the mother does admit that when overexcited he will not eat. Wilson begged her too not to talk to him about God—he already, she said, talked of God day and night.

*See Appendix C, page 155.

Letters cease, of course, when the Brownings arrive in London, a visit which probably sowed the seeds of the intense dislike of England later manifested by Pen. Elizabeth's father, in a violent letter to Browning, refused to see her, returning unopened all she had written to him over the years of their separation. Meetings with Arabel had to be surreptitious; Wilson's family lived in the north and must be visited by her. Despite the constant moves, there had been always in his life the stability of this little group of totally dedicated adults with abundant time to bestow on him. Now even his father was out of the house constantly, visiting his many friends, and the atmosphere surrounding mother and aunt, whether or not consciously perceived, must have affected so sensitive a child. His uncles ("mine untles") made much of him, and so did Elizabeth's old servants and humbler friends. But later from Paris Elizabeth wrote, "By the way dear Minny calls him 'Master Wiedeman.' Tell her he never was called 'Master Wiedeman' in his life before, and that for Minny to begin was too bad.... She must love him and call him Wiedeman."

It would be many years before Pen realized the class consciousness so rampant in the nineteenth century. But add together the climate, with its lack of sun, his mother's distress, however well concealed, the absence of Wilson making him fear that his mother would go next, at an age when weeks appear long months, and the general atmosphere of secrecy, nervousness, at moments even of terror, as the sisters achieved their meetings (he fancied that a "mitaine" dwelt in Wimpole Street), and one can imagine a sensitive and intelligent child perplexed and disturbed. Later in Paris his mother described him as remembering and protesting when he overheard them planning another visit to London.

For the moment he certainly recovered and on the journey to Paris which Carlyle and Elizabeth Browning have both recorded, Carlyle declared that Pen, who had been showing off furiously, had "as much enterprise as Napoleon Bonaparte."

The churches of Italy were ousted in his mind by the Tuileries Gardens and above all by the Punch and Judy shows. Despite an inability to pronounce certain letters —"I can" thus became "I tan"—he was fairly fluent in Italian and becoming so in English. Now he began to lisp in French and appeared undaunted over the problem ("apeau" he would say for his hat and "voila" he would exclaim at appropriate moments). The excitement of his life seemed constantly on the increase—sometimes stimulated by his mother's vanity. Invited to a party: "Robert says in his wisdom 'The child is too young for anything of the sort—he goes to bed at six—and you are a great deal too fond of pulling open rosebuds.... It's not good for the child and it's very foolish of you.'"

Obstinately she decided that Pen should "sleep at three and at seven he'll be wide awake again. So I shall have my way." Her "way" was largely the black velvet frock (13 francs a yard) cherry-coloured shoulder ribbons and "a tucker of my best lace."

Yet Wilson was already warning her of Pen's "supernatural singings and laughings in the middle of the night," which were she thought a species of hysteria. A few weeks later when he had a return of this, Elizabeth ran in and found him kicking "as if it were a slight convulsion," with eyes looking "like blue stars..." Now she *was* frightened, but although on more than one of these occasions they sent for a doctor, he never seems to have seen Pen at the bad moment.* The first time the child had "come in jumping and dancing," and the doctor called him "a fine little fellow." He did, however, advise the avoidance of excitement, and Wilson was told to take Pen no longer to Punch and Judy shows but to find quiet places for their walks. Yet in the very midst of these restrictions came his birthday with the usual splendid and exciting gifts, including from Wilson two magnetic swans "which he wouldn't believe were not alive. He got some bread for them directly."

There were too many other excitements in Paris besides Punch and Judy—and Elizabeth sends Arabel the letter Pen wanted to write to her "Dear Alibel, Penini see Napoleon pass—Plompity bebuffs, plompety bwans, plompity twumpets. Penini cwy Vive Napoleon. Napoleon take off apeau Penini."

Never did a child more need other children. When they came to play he was delighted, but the daily life remained that of an almost baby, centre and prime concern of a group of grownups, periodically over-excited and perpetually over-stimulated.

*See Appendix B, page 154.

Chapter Two

SMALL BOY

Back in Florence and just turned four, Penini said to Wilson, "Lily I want to peak to you a minute. I too large to be called Baby any more. I not lite you to say Baby. You muss say Penini." He told her too that *she* must speak English to him; he spoke Italian to the Balia and to his playmate Girolama (a poor little dwarf) but English to her and his parents. He was in fact already speaking each language separately, though his Italian remained the more natural, the better spoken. His mother was giving him regular brief lessons in reading and writing, and at the Bagni di Lucca, whither they repaired in the summer heat, were Edith and Joe, the children of William Wetmore Story, the well-known sculptor whose life Henry James would later write. Edith, though five years his senior, was an even greater friend than Joe—there was also Ferdinando, the Italian manservant, who became the greatest friend of all. He did conjuring tricks, creating cake which Penini believed to be produced by angelic powers. Marbles too had miraculously gone into his own neck and been recovered from his stomach. Pen at first announced that he had seen an angel catching the marbles and bringing the cake, but under pressure admitted that he hadn't actually *seen* the angel—only the marbles, and the cake, which was so good that his mother must tell him if people were coming to tea that Ferdinando might provide the wherewithal. Reading the Gospels, however, he was deeply interested in the miracle of the loaves and fishes—5000 was quite a number—but thought little of the water turned into wine. He had seen Ferdinando do that very thing.

Remembering that at this date Elizabeth had already begun her incursions into spiritualism and that Penini had been present at seances, one can hardly wonder that he took conjuring tricks in his stride. He says, Elizabeth had told Arabel a few months earlier, "a table in Pallis (Paris) says I am four years old." And after listening to a letter describing phenomena, his good-night speech was, "Well, dear Papa and Mama to-mollow morning let us hope the table will dance and pin (spin)." Elizabeth comments, "the 'let us hope' was magnificent. You see he is preparing to carry on the aspirations of his age." "Write for me little spillet," he implored another time, and the spirit obliged.

To a credulous mother was soon added a credulous nurse. Wilson, Elizabeth told Arabel a few months later, had had thrilling psychical experiences. Even Robert the unbeliever believed in her veracity. She had "felt herself in the midst of spirits... I didn't talk much about the subject to Penini—I don't want to excite him into trying experiments. I don't want him to write for long reasons. But he knows and believes in spiritual presences and manifestations and wouldn't be 'excited,' so as to be hurt by any manifestation of a kindly nature."

Whether Robert believed in Wilson's veracity or not was really irrelevant, as he has made clear enough both in his letters and in "Mr. Sludge the Medium." The element of reality was just what he feared most for his wife and would certainly have feared for their son. Luckily there was much else in the child's life, and this letter ends with the comment that Arabel may well think her sister extraordinary "in my programme of education with angels at one end and parties at the other."

Driving to Rome from Lucca, Pen sat in the coupé with Ferdinando, considering himself thereby a "toashman." But this was the first of their journeys that ended in deep unhappiness, for when they reached Rome, Joe Story had just died and Edith was in danger from a pernicious fever. Told that Joe had gone to heaven, Pen enquired as to whether Papa had seen the angels take him, and after some thought said slowly, "When I and Papa and Mama and Ferdinando and Lily go to God then we shall see Joe again." Followed a burst of tears and Wilson's wrath at his being upset—so young how could he understand, she said, but Elizabeth claimed he understood perfectly. And it was surely far better that he should look forward to a future meeting in heaven than be drawn into the idea of bringing Joe's spirit into their living room, with all the paraphernalia of darkness and mystery, raps and knocks.

Anyhow Edith was Pen's chief friend, and he was soon seen by Anne Thackeray pacing up and down outside the door of her sick room. He told her, she later said, "I sint you make a gleat deal too mush noise for Edith." Allowed into the room, he "sat by Edith kissing and patting her." Asked later if he liked Miss Sartoris, he said, "Not velly much. She tumbles up mine turls . . . I love only one durl and lat's Edith."

Later visits to England were a little better than the first but still fraught with nervous anxiety. Based on Paris in 1855, they were able to go over twice before returning the following year to Italy. Pen's uncles, George especially, had grown fond of him, and emboldened by previous success, Elizabeth seems to have taken him more openly to Wimpole Street. But she wrote to Henrietta: "Arabel deceived me into going when Papa was in the house. I understood that he was going out and under such circumstances of course I was in a constant state of nervous alarm. Think of Papa being absolutely caught the other day. George was playing in the hall with him [Pen] and he was in fits of laughter. Papa came out of the dining room and stood looking for two or three minutes. Then he called George and went back. "Whose child is that, George?" "Ba's child," said George. "And what is he doing here, pray?" Then without waiting for an answer, he changed the subject. To hear of it thrilled me to the roots of my heart. . . ."

The child had in fact begun to win his way with "mine untles." A twelve-year-old boy having mocked at his girlish appearance, Pen doubling his fists, described himself as saying, "Don't be impertinent, sir, or I will show you that I am a boy." His father and mother pointing out that the big boy could easily have killed him, Pen retorted, "Never mind, there would have been somebody to think of me who would have him hanged." "Great applause from the uncles," comments Elizabeth. And to the cousin he would later be with at Oxford, Henrietta's son Altham, Pen wrote "I go out in the streets almost every day with my sword and my gun and frighten all the people."

Besides London there was a melancholy visit to the sick (indeed dying) Mr. Kenyon at Cowes, when Pen "crept about like a small mouse," speaking under his breath. This was preceded by a few days with Arabel on holiday at Ventnor, when what can only be called a frantic consideration of Pen's day-to-day happiness shows itself in a letter to his hostess. Elizabeth writes pressing for "a line every day" from her sister. But she must not "tease him about writing" as the mechanical part calls for too much attention "when he has much play on hand." Let him be asked to dictate while she writes!

Though happy with this aunt, Pen liked England no better than before. Reaching Boulogne on their return, he said, "Do you see these houses? All white! Sint [think] of the dirty walls in London. Now I sint you don't want to go *bat* never."

Generously he admitted that she might want to do so "to see your flends," but he was far from sharing the wish.

Approaching his sixth birthday, Pen had begun, his mother said, to use hard words "entering a room," "preparing a table," "reposing his hands," doing things "gradually," "usually," and "suddenly." He was "velly solly to interlupt you," "quite glieved" to ask for another piece of candy. Brinsley Sheridan, who talked often of divine childhoods among the "blue blood" of England, had claimed never to have seen so lovely a child, and not merely lovely but remarkable for his "manners and learning"—an opinion which the mother told her sister was "very sound."

Before he was six Pen's mother had copied out for circulation among her friends some of his verse, noting the age at which each poem was written. A Mrs. Cowper having in 1856 asked to see some specimens of Pen's work, Elizabeth sent her these, saying nothing had been altered—they were wholly his. But in a later letter she admitted that she had suggested a very occasional word.

The Poem of Lucy Lee
by Penini—not six

1

Lucy Lee fell asleep,
    And everyone came round her,
And said 'Darling wings, darling wings'—
    Because she was a fairy.

2

She had naked arms,
    And naked little shoulders;
And everyone admired her
    Very much indeed—

3

Lucy Lee fell asleep;
    And all the people came
Every night, every morning—
    And still she kept asleep.

4

And her brother was very astonished,
    And very much alarmed;

And he thought she was dead,
    Because she kept asleep.

5

"Goodbye, goodbye",
    Everybody said,
When she kept asleep;
    "Goodbye, goodbye."

6

And twelve men came up,
    And put her in a cart,
And covered her up from the sun
    Nice and cozy.

7

And one ran by the side,
    To keep the clothes on,
Because the wind blew;
    And sang a beautiful song—

8

Poor Lucy Lee,
    With naked arms and shoulders!
She could not bear the cold
    In her dress white and red.

9

The song was, 'Cara Mia,
    'Cara mia piccina.'
Lucy Lee, Lucy Lee,
    Come bellina, bellina!

The Poem of the Willow Tree
(same age)

1

The Willow-tree
Is like a fountain,
But it doesn't make a noise.

2

But still the top of the tree,
And the fall of the branches,
Is very like a fountain.

3

It's Penini calls it a fountain,
Although he knows it's a willow-tree;
But still he calls it a fountain.

4

One day I saw it before;
Once at Rome,
And once again at Florence.

5

But no one called it a fountain;
No one at all that I know of,
No one at all except Penini.

6

I dare say there's a willow-tree
A willow-tree at Paris!
And Napoleon admires it very much,
And calls it a fountain, like Penini!

Small Boy | 21

Admitting that "the child has no application" though "vivid and quick to a degree," Elizabeth confesses (unwillingly?) one result of his upbringing: "He says sometimes 'I *tan* do whatever I like.'"

Yet there was a certain caution too. Pen loved to play with other children, but in Paris (now approaching his seventh birthday) he would not play with the children in the Tuileries Gardens till confident that his French was good enough. They had often invited him, and one day he said, "I wonder if it would make those little boys very happy if I went to play with them." There were several little girls, besides the now-absent Edith Story. Léocardie was "twite a darling with such bright eyes and beautiful turls." The concierge's little daughter, aged 5½, awakened an attachment "excellent for his French," but she did not want to be kissed, which Pen considered "very turious." At almost seven he was still, by his mother's rendering, apparently unable to pronounce certain letters in English. Probably the Italian fared better. But sharing a French lesson with Harriet, the maid of the moment, he flew into a passion when she had read ahead of him, "seized the book with flashing eyes" and threw it to the floor. His mother overheard him telling Harriet later that she was "twite the god of naughtiness. You're like the old Egyptians who—" But how she was like them remained unknown for at this point she interrupted him with the remark that *he* was like a naughty boy. Arabel must not of course believe any such thing: "you must not think he has grown naughty." And a line or two later: "Pen's poems are excessively admired in Paris I assure you. He made one for little May Sartoris on her birthday, which May (eleven years old) learnt by heart and goes about repeating—besides a magnificent ode on the war which has had its due renown."

The poem on the war is missing. But we have

>   To May Sartoris, on her birthday—
>   (Pen being seven years old)
>
>   1
>
>   It is May Sartoris's birthday,
>   This very day;
>   And here I've brought a present
>   For dearest, dearest May.
>
>   2
>
>   You are a flower, you are a flower,
>   For you are a May!
>   You are a May-Flower!
>   You prick us with thorns
>   At the jokes you make,
>   You make us scream and laugh.
>
>   3
>
>   I hope you'll laugh
>   And enjoy your birthday well—
>   I hope your pretty darling blossoms
>   Will be brighter than all others;
>   With beautiful silver flowers,
>   And beautiful golden thorns,
>   Dearest, dearest May.

On almost every birthday of his own Pen appears to have acquired some military toy—and then suddenly (at six) came a doll, which opened and shut its eyes, could be endlessly dressed, undressed and redressed, put to bed in a cot beside his own. His mother felt this a welcome change from pistols and cannons—and perhaps it was for her.

It was now March, 1856 and for his seventh birthday he had received a squirrel and a box of tools, kitchen utensils and a cannon, a nosegay of violets and a tricolor flag with an eagle. "Leally" he was "enchanted" by the flag and set out to display it in the Tuileries Gardens. And he was given the first day's holiday since he began lessons.

On the record goes—of lessons brilliantly successful when Pen's mood was right, dawdling and idling when it was wrong. The lessons prolonged one day in punishment, the pupil had one of his hysterical outbursts, threatening to kill himself, demanding a knife and accusing his mother of cruelty. It might almost have been better had she made up her mind occasionally to *be* just a little cruel. Yet while she could never have done this consciously, there was an unconscious cruelty in the strange system of lack of discipline and overburdening by knowledge. Pen appeared to absorb it all so readily. Languages, for instance: the Italians, says his mother, "consider him an Italian." One of them had commented on how good his English was for his age, and, adds Elizabeth, "the way he sets me down as a 'foreigner' is sometimes quite too funny." But when one learns that German had been added on top of the French begun so hopefully in Paris, the imagination reels. *Four* languages at nine years old—for Pen had certainly to work at learning English. It was not just the chattering that many a child can achieve as he hears foreign languages talked about him. He was learning also Geography and History.

The lessons were brief but when Elizabeth talks of only an hour and a half daily one can hardly suppose it covers Pen's translation of nearly two pages of Grimm's fairy tales, or such other "home work" as every teacher must allot. She talks in Paris, for instance, of "hearing" his French verbs before breakfast, after which Robert heard him spell. But she tells her sister, "He tears me to rags sometimes with his lessons ... inattention, talking nonsense, dawdling in finding his books ... and kissing me instead of pleasing me." Yet as she confesses in *Aurora Leigh*, these kisses were too a chief delight, as "The whole child's face / At once dissolves on mine."

Pen was naturally musical and loved to dance and play the tambourine when his father was at the piano. Music seems for a while to have become his favourite lesson. At six he could, according to his mother, read aloud the notes from a music book "quite fast." And Browning believed that if he pushed him he would "make an 'infant wonder' of him in two years."

Pen himself, not readily doubtful of his own abilities, felt it was "twite turious" that he was unable to accompany himself on the piano when singing "La donna e mobile." He did, however, to his own satisfaction, write an opera in Italian on Napoleon—his great hero—and the milkman—his enemy, who teased him by threatening to take away his gun. Written in Italian, to be sung by himself in that language, Napoleon's revenge for bad milk and cream served to his army was dramatic "e fusilado! e morto!" Finally came an equally dramatic burial, with music, noise and bells. Pen had heard and seen the famous actress Mrs. Sartoris and believed he, as an actor, was "rather lite" her.

But if this was fun, his father's teaching *and* the two and a half hours of concentrated practice insisted upon were, one fancies, pretty serious. Pen's own comment speaks volumes, "If I had a lady to teach me how very naughty I should be."

By eight years old he was also reading avidly. *Robinson Crusoe* given him for Christmas greatly delighted him, and he decided that St. John on Patmos must have been just like Crusoe. More surprising for his age was *The Count of Monte Cristo*—"Oh, magnificent, magnificent!" he cried, and was bent on reading the whole of Dumas. That he actually achieved his purpose of reading "Papa's favorite book, *Madame Bovary*" seems doubtful. Mayne Reid was certainly more suitable and Pen received one of his books with blazing eyes and the exclamation "Oh what fun."

Wilson had been for some time married to Ferdinando and there was now in Florence a little Romagnoli, named Orestes, loved by Pen "like a bruzzer" and nursed on his knees—to the terror of Elizabeth who thought it most dangerous. As her personal maid and Pen's attendant, "Lily," as Pen always called her, had been replaced by Annunciata, who gave him satisfaction on the whole. On her first arrival he was sick at Lucca with gastric fever. His mother describes him sitting up in bed looking like a wraith but exclaiming that his new maid "tells *novelle* quite finely! Stories of the devil and how he rides on a golden saddle with a silver bridle. Per Bacco!" But during the carnival he complained bitterly that Annunciata *would* hold his hand in the streets of Florence without wearing a mask. Carefully masked himself, how could he preserve his incognito: "Think of my position dear Mama."

The range of his grown-up acquaintance was wide, and, as his mother noted, free from any realization of class differences. For one birthday Annunciata "apprised" Elizabeth that Pen had bidden over twenty people ranging from his music master and wife to an old peasant living near by. His mother charged him with a message to Signora del Bene to say that it was only a children's party which Pen "assured" her he had delivered in a "gentlemanlike" manner. The Signora had to his bewilderment laughed and laughed, but, he said, he was certain she would be happy to meet this other guest. She knew her already and had even given her money.

Elizabeth's heart was with Pen in this ignoring of class distinctions, making it hard, she said, to explain them to him. She seems oddly enough not even to have tried— foolishly enough too in the world he would have to live in. For visibly poor people he had early shown compassion, asking for money to bestow on anyone who was asking for it. When in England he was away with Arabel, lamentations over his absence went up from servants as well as his parents. No amount of impishness seemed to diminish the charm felt by most of his contacts: the Abbé who presently taught him became as great a devotee as the Romagnolis, gruff old Landor called him Abelard with the five-year-older Edith cast for Héloise. And the Roman correspondent of an American paper, which had,

Elizabeth claimed, "gone like wild-fire from Georgia to Maine," had written "Those who know him best, love him most, not only for his parents' sake but for his own admirable qualities."

Elizabeth, with an honesty made easier by her conviction that Pen was essentially pure gold, describes his occasional fights with other children over their appropriation of his toys when he was host. But he was on the whole surprisingly good about yielding them up and very ready to kiss and make friends again after a skirmish.

He did demand, however, and usually got, full appreciation for these qualities and took offence at the criticism so readily offered by the adult world. A Miss Ogle, author of *A Lost Love*, having remarked, as he was offering her cake, that she had seen him "misbehaving on the Pincian," Pen was furious. Misbehaving! He had only frightened a "great girl," much "greater" than himself, with his toy pistol. Miss Ogle was not pretty (his parents had called her so), *he* would never call her anything but ugly, "She's my lost love." It was neat for a boy of ten, but he was, his mother said, growing more sensitive to being found fault with—especially by Robert, when there was trouble with the music. And although the Abbé soon won his way, Pen had called his mother "an *ungrateful creature*" for handing him over—she could have taught him Latin herself.

The hope that they would have lots of children was Pen's first thought when hearing of a marriage, and when he read the story of the twelve brothers he wished he had them, in which case "I shouldn't want Alessandro." Alessandro was a small Italian of Pen's own age with whom he played. But brothers were a real want, a real need.

Ferdinando was not quite as available as of old, though Pen had believed when he married that he would keep the promise he made that the boy's interests would always be first with him. To his horror even Ferdinando was left behind one year to mind the Casa Guidi with Lily. The couple had bought a house in Florence, but this was a commercial enterprise. Unfortunately Wilson must always be there to look after the tenants—especially when Walter Savage Landor had taken rooms there—with attendance. He was no easy boarder, and on occasion had thrown on the floor the dinner she had brought in a little late.

But it was a very bad arrangement—the frequent disruption of the Romagnolis' domestic life. Obviously they had been very happy that winter at the Casa Guidi, but for one to travel with the Brownings, leaving the other in Florence, did not work well. The first time Ferdinando was vexed and unlike himself, because Lily did not write enough; the second time Wilson's mischief-making sister told her of rumours concerning Ferdinando and Elizabeth's new maid, Annunciata. Both should have travelled—but how could they, first with a house and then with Orestes, the first-born, quickly followed by others. Elizabeth had an uneasy vision of a horde of travelling dependents. Surely the only answer was to leave Ferdinando behind with his wife. On one return to Florence Elizabeth was thoroughly frightened at finding Wilson in a state of religious mania. She begged her to desist for a while from reading the Bible, but the re-establishment of a steady domestic life was the real need.

All this seems to have gone over Pen's head. He loved them both dearly, but he was otherwise occupied in activities bringing important developments for mind and body. Siena was wonderful in the autumn: Pen "driving in the grape carts (exactly of the shape of the Greek chariots) with the grapes heaped around him—galloping through the lanes on a pony the colour of his curls," eating so many grapes he could eat nothing else, and reading Italian poetry to the pickers in the evening. The pony Robert had first hired and finally bought for him was a sturdy and beautiful little animal and travelled from Siena to Rome trotting beside their carriage. His father had done the buying and his mother commented that she was supposed to be the one who spoilt him!

Now he was riding it in Rome, his mother's great anxiety being that he should never ride with the young American sculptor Harriet ("Hatty") Hosmer—a close friend of both Brownings; she had, Elizabeth declared, been "thrown thirty times." The problem seems to have been solved by a groom whom visitors to Rome noticed riding with him. Pen, dressed by his mother with a plume in his hat, the skilful rider of a particularly beautiful pony (fed on oats and sedulously groomed), had become, he claimed, "one of the sights of Rome."

Getting near eleven, he had decided not to have toys for Christmas, but "a microscope instead and study nature." But after an expedition to a toyshop where his mother sent him to choose presents for other children his feeling changed. "I know it's foolish of me, Mama, but the shop looked so beautiful . . . and the *passionate* love of the old things came back to me, and I couldn't be *energetic* about the microscope any more." Now the present was to be a toy gun. "After all, you see Mama, I am *not* a man yet."

Less agreeably, but more important—his parents had as we have seen, secured a tutor for Pen, in lessons shared by Edith Story, a tutor who after taking up his office in Rome had accompanied them to Siena and introduced his versatile pupil to mathematics and the Latin language.

Pen's liking for priests had long faded under Ferdinando's influence. It was a bad moment for a church which had been in far too strong a position politically and financially. Sadly enough the genuine liberalism with which Pio Nono began his reign had passed away under the terror caused by the murder of de Rossi (his equally liberal minister) and the threat to himself. It was vital for Italy to be free from Austrian domination and to be welded into one country. At first Pio Nono had been acclaimed as the heaven-sent leader, but now patriotism and loyalty to him appeared to many Italians to be incompatibles. In a journal kept by Pen at Siena Elizabeth read, "This is the happiest day of my hole [sic] life for now dearest Vittorio Emmanuele is really nostro re." How would the Abbé take what Elizabeth describes as Pen's impertinent allusions to this ticklish situation, between himself as a priest and the small Italian patriot he was instructing? He took them well by leaving them without comment; indeed it was Elizabeth's impression that like many of the junior clergy, his heart was engaged in the unification and freedom of his country. He was glad, she thought, to escape onto the neutral ground of Virgil and a Latin Bible. Anyhow he, like all the rest, became Pen's devotee, and like Pen himself, said that the boy *could* do anything if he gave his mind to—or perhaps more accurately—set his will *on* his work and kept it there.

How much of what Elizabeth described was work actually done, how much just aspired to by the Abbé? "Think of this for one lesson. Forty Italian nouns to be turned into Latin in different cases. A page of Latin 'Sacred history' to translate into Italian. A Latin verb to write out— Three lines of Latin to *parse*. Besides *sums*."

The piano practice still continued for two hours, plus French *dictée* one day, geography or arithmetic another. "Then whenever there's a half hour free I seize on it to make him read German."

Appalling as all this sounds, a rather different light is cast by Pen's remark as he seated himself on the sofa beside Elizabeth, "Now Mama, let *us* do *our* verbs." She would look up words for him in the dictionary, was at his side to solve problems as they arose, and one can hardly doubt that Pen's kisses were an interruption as welcome to her as to him.

Pen's lessons may have proved a wholesome distraction in the blackness of what Elizabeth seems to have half-guessed were to be her last months on earth—but she told a friend how she could not of late look at him without a pang. Her beloved sister Henrietta was very ill—and the news of her death from cancer, although half-anticipated, came as an overwhelming blow. Should she, could she, have gone to England? But she would, she knew, have been worse than useless, she could only have suffered with Henrietta. She drew comfort in a correspondence with Harriet Beecher Stowe, who believed, as she did, in contacts with the dead through spiritualist manifestations. But a minor, yet deeply felt, blow was the discovery that another American friend, Sophia

Eckley, had been deceiving her—how is not quite clear, but she seems to have invented revelations to impress this easily impressed believer.

And then there was United Italy. Henry James felt that the intensity of her feelings, the way she would "flush and grow pale" over politics somehow diminished her—that she should be, to some degree at least, above the struggle "even in emotion and passion, even in pleading a cause and calling on the gods ... we absolutely feel the beautiful mind and the high gift discredited by their engrossment."

There were French regiments in Rome, for though Napoleon III was on the side of United Italy as against Austria, he had pledged France to the protection of the Papal States. Pen enjoyed the soldiers, marching beside them, talking to them in their own language—and we can fancy him coming home at night with a whole budget of information about his playmates—David Eckley and Italian boys as well. For Elizabeth writes to Henrietta of a party at the Duchesse de Gramont's at which "Pen wore a crimson velvet blouse and was presented to various small Italian princes—Colonnas, Dorias, Piombinos, and had the joy of talking ponies and lessons and playing leap-frog with them." Scions of the old Italian nobility were perhaps less likely to respond on the political issues in which Pen was so passionately interested. He had volunteered a contribution from his small pocket-money to be added to that of his parents towards the national struggle. For his father too, though deeply opposed to her spiritualism, was wholly with Elizabeth over the struggle for a free and United Italy. What he did not share was her admiration for the French Emperor, his opinion of whom we can read in *Prince Hohenstiel-Schwangau Saviour of Society*. He would not have published such a poem in Elizabeth's lifetime.

Although she had written to a friend of the pain she felt sometimes looking at Pen, the fear thus expressed had come—and gone—often enough before. She said once that she was always dying—yet never dead. Siena air or good news of the Italian cause brought such swift amelioration that fears were lulled. Perhaps Browning's own chief anxiety, besides the spiritualism, was the drug habit, which had been resumed though we do not know to what extent. The cough and weakness were alarming but came and went—almost always, it would seem, in response to mental and spiritual stimulants or depressants.

Rome was a more difficult city for an invalid than Florence or even Paris. The social life was intense among a group small enough for an outstanding conversationalist like Browning to be in tremendous demand, and Elizabeth was only too eager for him to be distracted from his exhausting care of her. There had been periods when he had sat up night after night—memories of the almost miraculous recoveries probably inducing a false sense of security.

Many were now the evenings when his father was out and Pen and Elizabeth were alone together. It is quite difficult to trace Pen's sleeping arrangements. As a baby Wilson had been the Nannie and he had slept in her room. On the frequent journeys one reads of anything—from Robert's dressing-room to the floor of their bedroom (a friend had rented this house for them and the struggle to get out of it took several months). At the Casa Guidi, changing from baby to small boy, Pen had a cot in the parental bedroom, and Elizabeth, describing how he had tied it to their bed, remarked that he was now too big (at eight) for this to go on. In Rome it was apparently resumed, and I tried in vain to reconstruct in imagination the Browning flat, now become offices. All we are told was that he went to his bed in the corner of a room, size unspecified.

Anyhow there they would talk by the hour until Pen was ordered—or coaxed—to leave his mother to her slumbers and dream himself of further adventures on his pony, of further admiring attention from visitors to whom the sights of Rome were pointed out—and he among them.

The last journey to Florence may have exhausted Elizabeth more than they realized. But what shattered her was the news that reached them in Florence of Cavour's death. Chief minister of Victor Emmanuel's government, he was the outstanding leader in the struggle for a free and United Italy. Without him all the forces he had contrived to unite would fall apart. Garibaldi? Pio Nono? Napoleon? One can see the names whirling through her fevered imagination—the cough shaking her anew. It was, she asserted, only one of her usual attacks, but Browning took alarm. The doctor came and went. Husband and wife were alone together, when, with all the love of her heart thrown open to him in words he could never repeat, she left him, smiling and beautiful as a young girl.

Pen was everything to his father in the days that followed. He was, said Browning, like *her*, as he gave the comfort he must sorely have needed himself. Their close friend Isa Blagden took him home with her that first night, leaving Browning alone with his dead wife. He shut a door in himself, says Chesterton, and "no one ever saw Browning again but only a splendid surface."

Was Pen an exception to this "no one"? I almost doubt it.

Child psychology was an unknown science in those days. The adult must do what was best for his children, but it is he and the friends from whom he seeks advice who know what that best is. There were of course obvious reasons for taking Pen to England: all his mother's near relations were there, his father's were in Paris and had never been willing or able to embark on the journey to Italy. The summer was coming on, which meant that Florence would become impossibly hot; they could join the Brownings by the sea in France.

So far this would seem an excellent plan—but it was far from ending there. Browning's strange abhorrence came into full force: he *could* not visit his father's house after his mother's death, later he could not even pass the house where Arabel had died in his arms. He *must* now get rid of Casa Guidi, and in all the years that remained he never again visited Florence.

But what did this mean here and now for Pen? Important citizens called to tell Browning how very happy they would be if the boy would remain as a citizen. And had he not often said "Sono Italiano"? Could it be good for him to follow the shock of his mother's death with the further shock of such an uprooting? Despite the constant travelling he looked on Casa Guidi as home—it was goodbye to Wilson and Ferdinando, to his playmates Alessandro and the Romagnoli children, to his music master and to the countless hangers-on whom he had bidden so joyously to his parties. Nor does it seem possible that all his belongings should be shipped to England, and at this stage they would at best have to wait until something other than comfortless lodgings could be found in London for him to have them again.

None of this does Browning seem to have considered: his letters are full of a deep anxiety as to whether he will know how to handle his now solitary task of Pen's education—yet he had no doubts about this first step, which involved also the disappearance of the golden curls, the outlandish dress, all that had marked a very unusual childhood. Pen, he said, was now a "common boy" (the word common meaning then only ordinary), and as such he could see to him personally. No need for the attendants that had hitherto surrounded their lives.

Much of this was obviously right, and would have long been done but for the mingled fears arising from Elizabeth's disease and her drug addiction. But how sudden it all was, how great a shock piled upon shock, as Pen said good bye to his more than nurse and her much-loved husband and children. He had once signed a letter to Wilson "Your everlasting Penini"—and he would show in later years that this was no idle boast.

His final sight in Florence is said to have been Walter Savage Landor throwing out of the window the dinner Wilson had cooked for him.

Chapter Three

THE ADOLESCENT

While the material is overabundant for Pen the baby and small boy, it becomes comparatively scant at adolescence. Not that his father did not mention him in his letters: there are well over two hundred references in the correspondence with Isa Blagden alone—but these paragraph references are far less illuminating to the outsider trying to look in than were Elizabeth's many pages in the letters to her sisters. Isa had been for years a close friend of both husband and wife. Browning had shared with her his moods of depression, whether over Elizabeth's failing health or his own sterility after the miserable reception of *Men and Women* by English critics and public alike.

Isa travelled with father and son as far as Paris, and a pact was made between them of monthly letters—she to write on the twelfth, the day of the Brownings' marriage, he on the nineteenth, the day they fled to France. Both kept this pact faithfully—a few days' lateness being matter for anxiety on either side. These letters are a chronicle of facts; there is little analysis and none of the quotations from Pen so abundantly supplied by Elizabeth.

A visit to Arabel was planned but abandoned. Passing through Paris together with Browning's father and sister, they reached St. Enogat, close to Dinard and at that date only a tiny village. Pen had learnt to swim long since in a summer at Le Havre and was now constantly in the water. The pony had come with them, and Browning walked himself "to death" for two hours daily, as no horse could be found for him and Pen must not miss his ride. Old Mr. Browning was devoted to children, as the Corkran sisters have testified: the drawings he made for them both, with pencil and brush, now at the University of Texas, are remarkable, and Alice Corkran tells the story of his skill and patience as a teacher. All this was poured out on his grandson, and Browning declares that Pen's "loud merry laugh is never out of my ears." The father was in fact amazed at his son's power of adaptation to new circumstances. Yet he had had to adapt often enough already, and it was certainly one of his strong suits.

These summer holidays would always remain a bright period in the new and strange existence that Pen was entering when they turned their backs on Europe for an England he had always hated—black, wet, dull and lonely. Browning in his deep grief was wholly devoting himself to the child whose likeness to his wife increased the father's already deep affection. But also he had forbidden himself for a time all normal social distractions. After a resolute and successful fight to get a horse-box for Pen's pony hooked onto their train, he saw and avoided Tennyson at Amiens. A little later, meeting him in Kensington Gardens, Anne Thackeray felt that he was shrinking from even old friends. "He was in a jarred and troubled state and not himself as yet."

One can imagine what his aunt Arabel must have meant to Pen—indeed what this sister must have meant to Browning. The simplicity with which he had accepted even the brothers who had at first so almost savagely refused to accept him is an endearing trait. Much later Pen's wife would note that he never used the word "in-law." And just as she would become his daughter, Arabel was always for Browning a very dear sister. For the rest of her life he visited her daily, and we can hardly doubt that Pen found in her some shadow at least of the mother he had lost, that he poured out to her the feelings, pent up or pushed aside, in the months of seaside air and exercise and healthy fatigue followed by deep sleep.

Arabel was far more concerned about the surrounding poverty than were the rest of her family—or indeed than the Brownings, and her life was, as we have seen, devoted to what were known as "ragged schools."

A pompous but moving article by Lord Shaftesbury in the *Quarterly Review* of December 1846 had praised these schools,* opened, he said, by "excellent persons in humble life who went forth into the streets and alleys," inviting "these miserable outcasts to listen to the language of sympathy and care." He described the derelict children in grotesque rags looking for flotsam from the river, going "home" to a hovel with a cesspool at the door, sleeping six or more in one bed or on a pile of rags. "Happy is the family that can boast of a single

---

*Quoted in *Their First Ten Years* by Marion Lockhead, (London: John Murray, 1950).

room to itself, and in that room a dry corner." All this in Lambeth and Westminster (the two worst districts) "within a walk of our own dwellings."

Pictures of the period show these children sometimes in the fantastic remnants of smart dresses, sometimes covered by a coarse bit of sacking. "The wind," said a report on Glasgow in the forties, "showed the lightness of the garments . . . and the ease with which it could pierce to their very bones." London was rarely quite as cold as Glasgow, but Lord Shaftesbury used almost stronger terms describing the miserable condition of the pale and feeble children going home to "depositories of death" within a walk of his well-to-do readers. The ragged schools were, he felt, assisting in a task which he appealed to the wealthy to accomplish—"raise them to a level on which they may run the course which is set before them, as citizens of the British Empire and heirs of a glorious immortality."

"This grows curiouser and curiouser," commented Alice on the far less odd surroundings in Looking Glass Land.

It would be interesting to know how curious it looked to Arabel. The pious people of her class were more inclined at that date to quote the text "the poor you have always with you" than to dwell on the parable of Dives and Lazarus, which might well have frightened them to death.

One wonders certainly how much, if at all, Arabel talked of her work to Pen. Not having her letters to Elizabeth, one can only guess—but my guess is that with friends or relatives she rarely dwelt on the dominant concern of her own existence. One would imagine her haunted by what she had seen and heard all day. Yet after reading a good deal on the period and looking at such illustrations as a small well-dressed girl encountering another, bareheaded, carrying a broom wherewith to sweep the crossing in a winter street, one can only ask what use this or any other reminder was to the ruling class. Even if such pictures were shown, it was to stimulate generosity, but with no idea of awakening shame. Wealth and abject poverty side by side had come to appear of the nature of things, and Mr. Podsnap was not the only Londoner who repudiated as a calumny the known fact that many died of starvation in the streets of London. *He* was living in an England in which this was impossible!

Whether or not Arabel talked with Pen on a topic which Elizabeth's letters confirm one in feeling she kept apart from her family life, she certainly had both sympathy and a degree of leisure to bestow on her nephew.

His days must have been very different from the casual existence of Casa Guidi. Conceive of an English household after the life—not merely Italian, for that too could have been to some extent formal—but definitely gypsy, that he had lived for so many years. One wonders if he tried talking to the well-trained manservant as if he were Ferdinando, or what he made of the cook-housekeeper, both of whom would tell reporters later of Browning's great merits as their employer. It is quite possible that he, like many Victorian children, did have the freedom of the servants' hall. But I rather doubt it.

Mrs. Orr's defence, in her biography of Browning, of Pen's having been allowed to play with the little Italian peasant Alessandro—who suddenly, to his delight, turned up one day in London—suggests a regrettable snobbery on her part, but it suggests also that Pen was terribly short of playmates.

All this was secondary to the profounder question of a nationality. Holidays were all very well, Pen had already spent enjoyable ones in France and endurable ones in England. But he thought of himself as Italian where his father was to the core an Englishman. Browning had sacrificed much when for the sake of his wife's health he gave up his own country; his moods of nostalgia for Italy were chiefly one aspect of his longing for her. Florentine worthies had offered citizenship to Pen which Browning had refused. "I distrust," he wrote to Story, "all hybrid and ambiguous natures and nationalities and want to make something decided of him."

Was it not too late to make this eager little Italian into a "decided" Englishman? And if it was to be done, surely the wisest course was not the one chosen—education at home with a tutor.

The decision was not taken lightly. Letters to many of Browning's friends, especially to Isa Blagden and William Story, are filled with what was for him a chief preoccupation—Pen was now thirteen and the obvious thing appeared to be sending him to one of the famous schools of England—Winchester, Eton or Rugby. But Browning shrank from this, wisely perhaps, realizing that his sheltered childhood had in no way prepared Pen for the rough and tumble of a public school (so England denominates these expensive, selective establishments). He wrote to Story that a tutor, he had been told, was really better at bringing a boy on than was a Public School—

The Adolescent | 43

"The advantage of Eton is *not* of getting scholarship, but of—of—of—why getting aristocratic connexions and friendships, which in England is the chief end of man." He had, however, another reason—and that a far less reasonable one. He did not want to abandon the many elements in Pen's education not needed for Oxford. Classics must of course be primary, but "German, Drawing, Dancing, and such other matters, as much as he can properly bear" must not be given up. In another letter to the same correspondent, William Story, music is added to this list—and both French and Italian. Greek, Latin and Mathematics were the essentials for the University. Among Pen's physical activities were swimming, skating when the weather was propitious, riding and fencing, which he and a friend Willie Bracken learned together. And he rowed regularly on the canal beside the house.

It sounds an incredible programme, but even more astonishing are the references to an adult social life which had begun on quite a scale by the time he was fifteen. "I do go to balls," writes Browning to Isa in February 1863 (Pen being a month short of his fifteenth birthday)—"when Pen goes, as was the case last week at Lady de Grey's; and he would go to another tomorrow but for the cold—the same reason keeps him from accepting an invitation to dine with Lady Westmorland tonight and go to Fechter" [a famous actor of the period].

On March 10th Pen was taken by Lady de Grey to see "from the War Office in Pall Mall" the illuminations in honour of Princess Alexandra of Denmark's marriage with the "Crown Prince"; Sir Edward Lytton had invited father, son and tutor to Knebworth for Whitsun; but though "he really pressed it," Browning refused—not even "with the Archangel Gabriel" would *he* spend a week "at his country seat." On May 19th the father boasts that Pen "figures everyday in Rotten Row, and only yesterday somebody wrote to me saying how much his horsemanship is noticed." And he saw the Ascot races that year from a friend's house.

On January 19th, 1864 "a bitter week" had struck London "to Pen's delight, who bought skates at once and used his time fully." Too fully perhaps, for the letter goes on to say that Pen "in common with all the world" has caught a cold. Whenever this happens it is chronicled, and one realizes how uneasy any father would be about this particular mother's son. In almost every letter to the sympathetic Isa comes a record of Pen's state, physical and intellectual. "He continues to do very well, putting increased interest into his various business: I am very glad in the hope that he will get scholarship, accomplishments, health—and be happy and indulged all the same." Although reassuring Isa that he would never become a monomaniac about Pen's education, the father confessed that "if he were not here I should be nowhere." The concentration was certainly intense, the affection profound.

By November, 1864 the sixteen-year-old has "dreadfully incipient mustachios." But a month later Browning is showing for the first time some anxiety about his own programme. "I have been trying an experiment, you see, in resolving to *broaden* his acquisitions, instead of *deepen* them in one or two respects, to the detriment of all the rest." Had he cut off modern languages, drawing and music, Pen would now be ready for Oxford. The father

The Adolescent | 45

and the son too were becoming alarmed about Balliol standards. "I was to have talked over all these troubles with Jowett," Master of Balliol College. But Jowett's ambition for a scholarly college was intense, and he would perhaps have failed to contradict the absurd report father and son had heard that entry to Balliol was nearly as difficult as graduation from any other college!

Yet the social distractions still went on. In March 1864 his father writes of Pen's going to the Oxford and Cambridge boat-race "in the boat which is expected to hold the Prince of Wales." And a year later, "Pen is quite well again. Was 16 on the 9th ult. A great boy—or rather young man—I took him to a party last Monday, and, woe's me, he figured in coat and white tie."

Was not the father doing with the adolescent precisely what he had entreated the mother not to do with the child?

But very, very gradually Browning was admitting doubts and fears at least about the proportion of various elements in his son's life and character. "His whole soul," he wrote in March 1866, "is concentrated on the approaching Oxford and Cambridge boat-race,—which I have no objection to." But a year later: "Pen *boats*—cares more for that than aught else,—unless perhaps for shooting and breech-loaders: but he is a good fellow all the same and may wake up ambitious one day."

An odd thing had happened to the child who had so often said, "I can do anything," for his tutor was now reporting him as lacking in self-confidence and doing in consequence less well than both his powers and his knowledge warranted. He was of course no longer supported by the atmosphere of admiration built up by his mother, the Abbé, Edith Story, Wilson and Ferdinando, even Annunciata—all united in thinking him the most marvellous of boys.

In one of the analyses he often sends to Isa of Pen's character, Browning uses a surprising word. He describes Pen as "good, kind, cautious, self-respecting and true." At what point did the impetuous child become a *cautious* young man?

But the father's adoration took as one of its forms an unfortunately perfectionist attitude, with his own views in the forefront concerning the type of perfection desirable. Browning never seems to have asked himself what type of perfection was accessible to the type of child he had happened to father. Victorians indeed never thought in such terms: a child was a child, lessons were lessons, father knew best. Browning's own father had been a wiser man, and the poet himself was misled by Pen's innate wish to please and a much higher degree of adaptability than his own genius would have made possible.

There was, too, another element never mentioned but surely not negligible. It is not infrequent for a very lovely child to turn into a rather plain man, and plain Pen certainly did become. By his later teens no one could have written such a description as did Mrs. Hawthorne in the Florentine days. Meeting him first in the passage, she saw Pen as "a waif of poetry, lovelier still in the bright light of the drawing room." Waiting on them at tea, he was "graceful as Ganymede."

Nathaniel wrote even more surprisingly, "I never saw such a boy as this before, so slender, fragile and spirit-like,—not as if he were actually in ill health, but as if he had little or nothing to do with human flesh and blood. His face is very pretty and most intelligent, and exceedingly like his mother's. He is nine years old, and seems at once less childlike and less manly than would befit that age. I should not quite like to be the father of such a boy, and should fear to stake so much interest and affection on him as he cannot fail to inspire. I wonder what is to become of him,—whether he will grow to be a man,—whether it is desirable that he should."

We are reminded that Pen's health was as perpetual a source of anxiety to his father as it had been to his mother, though growth and an immense amount of air and exercise were diminishing the concern of earlier years. But we would dearly like to know when and how the astonishing change took place in his appearance. Probably it came very gradually, and of course people do not notice a teenage boy as they do a lovely child of whichever sex. Nor could his father ever have realized that a boy so like the wife he had adored could be called other than beautiful. In her lifetime a description of her exquisite mind but plain appearance had driven him into a kind of frenzy. But by the time Pen could be called an adult he was certainly a plain one, a minor element perhaps in shaking his self-confidence.

It was only when Pen got to Oxford and passed from his father's influence that the new boy, mentally as well as physically a young man, appeared on the scene.

He had of course been waiting in the wings, and Browning had unwittingly made everything ready for him. When Jowett advised postponement for a little longer concentration on his Greek (his Latin being "up to the mark"), Pen's father took lodgings for him in Oxford—and provided him with a boat of his own! Browning wrote to Isa with great satisfaction both of invitations from important people and of the success of the "good look" Pen was taking into the lives of "young men given to study."

One feels that Pen may quickly have learnt the value of telling his father what his father wanted to hear. He must almost certainly have already been playing billiards with perhaps rather different young men from those "given to study." He won a gold cup for his skill at this game. There were, too, yet other young men to be met as he plied his oars on the river.

Jowett's identification with his College was total. I doubt whether even his own enthusiasm for Browning's poetry would have rated for the poet not merely an honorary degree, but a fellowship with a room of his own in the College, had he not realised it would bring kudos to Balliol. The man parodied as saying

> "First come I; my name is Jowett.
> There is no knowlege but I know it.
> I am Master of this college:
> What I don't know isn't knowledge"

might have hesitated to admit even the son of a genius and a friend, who failed to meet Balliol's exacting standards. The decision rested not with him but with his examining board, but letters at Baylor University show how anxious he had been to help Browning. He did not at first despair of Pen's becoming fit for the Oxford of that date, at which Classics were literally everything. In Latin reading Pen was "quite up to the standard of

The Adolescent | 49

matriculation at Balliol and nearly up to the mark in Latin writing." But in Greek he was far behind.

Finding in him "very good sense and good abilities," Jowett felt he should come to Oxford, but the preparatory programme proposed for the next nine months was surely something to make that young man shudder.

> I have told your son what I think he should do in the next 9 months. Read 12 books of the Iliad and 12 of the Odyssey and know them.
> Read 4 books of Thucydides
> 3 books of Livy.
> Write an English Essay every week—translate and retranslate and then learn by heart a few lines of Cicero daily. I would recommend him also to translate a few lines of English into Latin and of Greek and Latin into English daily without a Dictionary—Viva voce.

This was written in April, and in December Jowett, while approving the way in which Pen was "repairing his deficiencies," added another warning note: "I find him very intelligent, but unused to writing in English and also deficient in memory."

Despite all efforts Pen failed twice in the postponed examination. But after further work at home he was admitted by Jowett to one of his reading parties during the Long Vacation. This was a singular privilege for a boy not yet at the University, and it also enabled Jowett to understand better the mind of one whom as a person rather than a pupil he clearly found attractive. What had puzzled him most was the possibility "that while he can do really difficult things he may fail utterly in the easiest ... I believe that, what most people complain of, is a real defect in him—a weakness of memory—

which is not to be taken at all as a measure of his abilities ... I do not think he is at all to blame for he has been very industrious but he is not able to muster more than a certain amount of interest and attention."

Jowett advised that the effort for Balliol should still be made and told Browning he even hoped for success—he had said no word either to Pen or to the Fellows, whose decision he would not attempt to influence. This letter was written in October, 1868, but in September he had written to Florence Nightingale: "I am grieved about young Browning who I fear can never be made to pass his examination at Balliol. He is a clever fellow yet he forgets [Greek] quicker than he learns it."

So, to his father's bitter disappointment, Pen did not get into Balliol. But he did pass creditably into Christ Church and his tutor told Browning how puzzled he was over the earlier failure, which he attributed to nervousness, Jowett to carelessness. For Christ Church there were, Browning wrote triumphantly, "Two dozen *postulants*, and eleven recipients only, as these ritualistic asses would say"—and Pen was one of the eleven.

It was a good year from his point of view—and at first, from his father's, who watched delightedly when the Christ Church boat with Pen as cox "bumped" five times. For American readers this may need explaining: the rivers Isis at Oxford and Cam at Cambridge are both too narrow for side by side racing, so the boats start in the order in which last year's race left them. When the boat of one college draws near enough for its bow to touch the stern of the other it is said to bump and will be ahead of it in the next race. Browning and Sarianna, watching the race, felt they had never seen Pen "at such advantage, at least in his *manly* character." But alas the "manly character" would in the end mean for Browning the disappointment of his very unreasonable hopes for a son who, despite many talents and much charm, was simply not an intellectual.

And he was now being encouraged by his surroundings to indulge that social weakness which Browning had perhaps not fully faced in himself and of which he had almost certainly failed to warn his son. Later his own poetry suffered from it, but at this date he had it under control. *The Ring and The Book* appears to have been written chiefly in the early morning, but Pen had not learnt to burn the candle at both ends. His long vacation did not include a reading party as it had the previous year, or, if it did, Browning does not mention it to Isa. But in September he answers a question from her as to why he had been sounding worried. "My 'worry' has increased to pretty nearly the last degree, but there is no need to put it down on paper yet—or perhaps ever—so, only be prepared to 'comfort' me when there is absolute need."

Yet he could not but enjoy his son's enjoyment, including his social success—in which good shooting and skill at billiards were not negligible elements. Browning and Elizabeth had agreed in hating field-sports, indeed Browning has written a poem about which one wonders —was it forced from him after a letter to Isa that summer, "Pen has got what he wanted—shooting and deer stalking ... shot a splendid stag-'royal,' the head of which will glorify his rooms at Ch. Ch." His aunt Sarianna in a letter to a friend describes more fully this "great event" in her nephew's life. The hunt had gone on from morning to night and a search party had actually been organised to look for Pen, when he came in "radiant with delight." He was, said his aunt proudly, the only successful huntsman and he received compliments from all—including the keeper.

"A splendid Stag royal." Just such an animal faces in the poem a huntsman on a narrow path above a precipice,—so narrow that as sole hope the man lies down, the stag very carefully walks over him. Both are safe—but the man cannot resist the kill.

> I dare to place myself with God
>   Who scanned—for He does—each feature
> Of the face turned up in appeal to Him
>   By the agonizing creature.

Man and stag fall together but though the huntsman is damaged for life he can still win applause and a round of drinks as he tells his story. It was a true story, told to Browning, though Pen would never have acted thus. He, like all the Brownings, loved animals (strange ones too, Browning followed by a toad round his mother's garden, Pen carrying a snake in his pocket and filling his house with loud-mouthed birds). Field sports are something else, and many people who loathe and abominate vivisection would (like Chesterton) defend killing in sport. Browning in theory would not. Pen was in a specialized compartment of his father's being, but that being was surely shaken between the glorifying of his son's walls and the murder of a stag.

To what extent had Pen been hit by the social atmosphere of Oxford—especially perhaps that of such a college as Christ Church? It is exceedingly difficult for anyone who did not live even for a short period through the heyday of England's social snobbery to realise what it meant. The dropping of the word "gentry" may be called a land-mark. For the large section of the population covered by it would have been utterly horrified to be told they were "middle class"—and the middle class astonished to be described as gentry. The grouping by Chesterton of my mother and himself under the former designation was enjoyed as a huge joke by many of her friends. I remember serious discussions with cousins of my own as to whom we were allowed to "know," and considerable perplexity as to how to behave in what should have been quite simple situations. Two friends of ours who travelled a lot thought it only fair to continue in London acquaintanceships made abroad, but told us of people who would cancel them totally on returning home.

Landowners were for long called "landed gentry"; gentry too were the clergy, officers in the army and navy, the vast multitudes who had titled relatives, etc. But large as the class of gentry was it was intensely exclusive, its members refusing to "know" socially anyone below their own fairly clearly drawn line.

Browning's grandfather was said to have kept an inn. This might exclude him—but far worse, because closer and more recent, was his *father's* employment as a clerk. And even if he, by his poetry and his social gifts, had crossed the line, the admission of his son might have remained more than doubtful. About this Browning seems to have been far too greatly concerned. Never in the letters to Isa does he suggest that his son's social engagements may endanger the Oxford degree which mattered so much. It is possible that they were not as frequent as mentions in the letters suggest; but surely they began far too early and balls must, for instance, have added to the fatigue of the day's study.

It would have been on the social side that Pen was "cautious." He had probably discovered snobbery in London, even as the son of a father so popular as almost to have overcome it. "Almost," yes, for down to the end of his life the favourite description by those who happened to dislike him, Julian Hawthorne, for instance, was that Browning was "not a gentleman."

Although Belloc once said that he remembered the day when a poet or indeed any writer of distinction was coveted even more than a duke by the hostess planning her dinner party, this was probably only true in some circles. But in Browning a hostess had secured both a celebrity and a conversationalist so entertaining that her chief trouble was to get any of his company in her drawing-room after dinner.

Husbands often neglected to say, "Shall we join the ladies," and instances are recorded of the butler sent more than once to remind the host that they were waiting. (Would Women's Liberation be more angry with the host who monopolized, or the women who coveted, the society of a poet who was still a mere man?)

Pen's holidays spent abroad and a social life under his father's aegis were, however, slight preparation for an Oxford where "gold tassels" were within men's memories on the caps of the aristocracy, at a College moreover frequented by them. Important intellectuals like Jowett himself were kind to Pen and wanted to help him as his father's son—and so, probably, would the "reading" element in his or any other college, for it was the period when, as Browning noted, the young were discovering the poetry overlooked or disparaged by the critics.

But Pen was not seeking readers as his friends. He found these more agreeably through billiards and rowing—and, again, probably this had begun in the months before his official entry into the university. There has to be a good deal of guessing and of reading between the lines, however frequent Browning's mentions are of his son. But besides the word "cautious," it is surprising to find "undemonstrative" in Browning's descriptions of this new Pen.

Arabel appears at first to have been the only Barrett in close relations with Browning. He was on good terms with George, but an uneasy note can be heard in some of the letters. Someone had apparently muddled a matter of re-investing Pen's money, and the wrath Browning pours out is altogether disproportionate: one feels he half-feared George might be blaming him.

Again, while nothing distressed—and enraged—him more than any personal allusion to Elizabeth appearing in print ("their paws in my bowels," he once called it), such allusions were suspected by some Barretts to be inspired by him. Many, many years later, when Jeannette Marks visited old Mr. Barrett's great-grandson in Jamaica, she listened with amazement to his defence of the paternal rejection of Elizabeth. Browning was "not a gentleman." His grandfather had been an innkeeper.

But why, Miss Marks asked, had both his own great-grandfather and Henrietta been cast off too in consequence of their marriages? That was explained readily enough: both were marrying second cousins and the relationship was too close to be desirable. It is impossible to read this without a broad smile, remembering the ostracism maintained up to the father's death, extending to Elizabeth's only child, remembering that all three offenders were cut out of their father's will and that he refused to see any of them again. Old Mr. Barrett *may* have been a snob, but what this conversation showed most clearly was that his great-grandson was one. And when one later hears some Barrett views of the adult Pen, it is well to bear this in mind. He was never wholly forgiven for being a Browning. But the criticisms that have survived belong mostly to a much later date and represent therefore a later generation talking about a much older Pen.

With most of the Barrett brothers Browning himself was now on good terms, and in a long letter to Isa he tells, as typical, a story of Quixotic generosity and indifference to financial loss which he terms characteristic of the family. Obvious lacunae in their make-up were to a large extent the result of the strange education which had failed to crush Elizabeth: as Jeannette Marks points out, only this physically battered woman made her escape from a mental battering that had left its mark on them all. Pen's heritage on his mother's side was a curious one—but again has gone unnoticed as an element in his development.

His tutor's report for Pen's first term listed all the subjects he was reading and concluded "very regular." But in the second term though translation was "sufficent," Latin prose was not, Virgil hardly, and some quite illegible subject was labelled "fere nil"—practically nothing.

The result of too much boating and billiards was all too manifest. Altham Surtees, Henrietta's son, was at

The Adolescent | 57

Christ Church with Pen, and an extract from his father's diary for November 25th, 1869 ran "Our darling Altham, this day, passed his preliminary exam for 'smalls' (as they call it) at Ch. Ch. Oxford. Thank God. His cousin Pen (Robert Barrett Browning) also of 'the House' ploughed poor fellow the same time."

A curious little interlude between Pen's repeated failures as a student is indicated in one of Browning's monthly letters to Isa Blagden.

"What do you suppose," he wrote, "what that should, most of all imaginable, stupify me?" Pen had "broken into violent poetry." *As* poetry his father thought little of it, "but considering the boy's all but absolute ignorance of poetry, it is a very welcome proof indeed of what may still be in him."

This was early in 1879, in the spring of which Pen seems to have woken from a dream-life of sport and social activity into the grim reality of his Oxford situation. But ten final weeks of feverish activity under Mr. Gillespie left him in so high-wrought a state as almost to ensure failure. The uncle's journal for June 14th, 1870 reads: "Poor Pen—again ploughed for smalls." Once more Gillespie proclaimed nervousness as the main cause, but with one of his almost predictable reactions Browning fell into despair. He seems to have realised in one act the idleness and the extravagance which had marked the first two years of Pen's release from leading strings too long kept on.

He had spent, Browning told George Barrett, about £170 in a term which had run only five weeks! In a later letter the estimate was reduced to £150—or £160, but it was for those days an enormous sum; and Pen, no longer the docile child of yore, announced that he would not consent to live at Christ Church on less money —adding that to gain a First Class seemed to him "no great thing." And all this in front of Uncle "Occy."

Browning's cry of despair to George Barrett was at least as unreasonable as Pen's reaction. In a first frantic letter he talks of his own last ten years as wasted and of the same period as one of complete idling by Pen—what can he do but pension his son off to live in the country? The diplomatic career would be expensive and fruitless, the army, abhorrent to himself, would have been still more so to Elizabeth. Had George been still a practising barrister he would have begged him to take Pen under his wing. As it is, "What am I to do?"

A main revelation of this letter is of the poet's own unfitness to cope with life in the world to which he had returned, after fifteen years of devotion to one purpose in a climate created by himself and the other poet who was his wife. What *had* he thought of for Pen after the Oxford years?—for surely he had not dreamed of a continuing academic life. He seems to have felt as helpless as the young man himself. The desk in an office which he recognised as unthinkable left no alternative but the life of idleness Pen was already pursuing with considerable verve. Many "country seats" were open to him when London palled.

It was no such disgrace in those days as it became later for a young man to be known chiefly as a valuable adjunct at country house parties. Pen shot well, danced well, played the piano well—and billiards too. He was a good oarsman and fisherman. At this stage of his life he seems to have been gaining in social popularity

The Adolescent | 59

both generally and with his cousins. With Altham Surtees he was always on excellent terms. A letter from Sarianna to her friend and Browning's, Annie Egerton Smith, speaks of a visit to his "Uncle Occy." In another letter he is in Scotland with relatives he had not known before "but who have taken a great liking to him (all the Barretts are very clannish)." It was at this Barrett home that Pen met Millais and Sarianna wrote of his going grouse shooting and deer stalking and salmon fishing with the painter. On one occasion they caught three salmon each and "the event" was put in the paper. He had beautiful manners and is mentioned by Mrs. Drew (Gladstone's daughter) and Lady Ritchie (Anne Thackeray) as coming to their assistance when a street must be crossed or a cab obtained. Put up later for a London club, he got an overwhelmingly large vote. He made, as far as one can learn, no enemies. He was already twenty-one, and his mother's small fortune was probably at his disposal, his father's house open to him as a base. But of course he continued to run up many bills which Browning lamented but duly paid.

That curious couple writing jointly under the name of Michael Field, a young aunt and her niece, rumoured to have a Lesbian streak in their relationship, described Pen as "jocund" when he appeared at the paternal luncheon table. He seems to have been amusing as well as easily amused. "He is unfit," his father had written to George Barrett, "for anything but idleness and pleasure —each as harmless as such indulgences can be."

The editor of these letters asks in a footnote whether this means that Browning was unaware, complacent, or incredulous of the rumour that before he was nineteen

Pen had had two illegitimate children by Breton peasant girls. He does not raise the question of evidence, for which others besides myself have sought. It could of course quite easily be true. These things happen at all dates, in all societies. Pen's mother had foretold that in his teens he would experience some passionate love affair. But evidence is missing. A friend told me he had visited the villages concerned and learnt nothing. Nor do we get a hint in Browning's letters, now open to the world with none of the omissions so long making published letters worthless for the investigation of private matters. Even an account book of Browning's has been published and analysed. And the story was never uncovered by the famous sleuth who laid bare so many details of Pen's as well as Browning's life, Frederick Furnivall.

Jowett is parodied as saying, "What I don't know / Isn't knowledge." This could almost without parody be said of the co-founder of the London Browning Society, the expert on early English texts, whose insatiable curiosity did in fact at times embarrass Browning. Yet—there's no smoke without fire, and that smoke may drift with uncanny indirection. Twenty years later it would drift to Asolo.

There was anyhow enough to worry the poet for the next three years, and it is amazing how calmly but helplessly he seems to have taken it after his first outburst. His sister Sarianna had come to keep house for him after their father's death, and father, aunt and son were apparently a happy trio. But nothing was attempted to give Pen a fresh start.

The Adolescent | 61

What happened at this time—or earlier, or later—to the religion of Elizabeth Barrett's intensely religious child? Although Browning's own faith is manifest in his poetry, it was from his mother chiefly that Pen had imbibed the Christian message, as indeed he had almost all his childhood impressions. His early love of things Catholic, arising from beauty both visual and oral, had been shaken by Ferdinando's bitterness towards the official church. It seemed obvious enough that greed for temporal power was the greatest barrier against United Italy, which had become both Ferdinando's dream and that of this small Italian patriot. If Pius would have relinquished the States of the Church he would have kept many more of the souls who inhabited them. It is one of the saddest stories in Church history, and it is hard today to enter into the minds of men who felt sincerely that by giving up the lands which had become the "Church's patrimony," they would be betraying the Christ who had nowhere to lay his head.

Then too Ferdinando appears to have been subjected to an astonishing sort of espionage: he told the Brownings that not to go to Confession at least yearly put him under suspicion. He married Wilson at the British Embassy in Paris, since it would have been harassing—indeed almost impossible—for a man in his position to obtain the necessary permits to wed a Protestant—and they were in a not uncommon hurry. All this I can readily believe: the bureaucracy of both State and Church can be intolerable, and in Italy they were united. Pen, with his love for Ferdinando, must have realized enough to make organized religion suspect to him, and it is impossible to tell whether his mother's really intense love of God had reached and affected him after the early childhood in which it had meant so much.

Browning's Christianity was, I think, less vivid than Elizabeth's except at such moments as after his mother's death, when he wrote the marvellous *Christmas-Eve and Easter-Day*; Arabel certainly believed as deeply as her sister. When Pen got to Oxford, compulsory chapel was still the rule, but one wonders which way it drove the students thus compelled.

There is no sign of the presence of religion in Pen's later life—but there is no sign of its absence either. What does turn up again and again is the dislike for the Church of Rome first sown by Ferdinando. A curious correspondence with his father arose later from one of Pen's pictures—a monk reading a more than doubtful book—which Lehmann had bought and wanted to exhibit. Pen was already against this, feeling it to be one of his less successful efforts, but his father urged in a lengthy letter that the decision must be based on the *subject* of the picture.

"Hating priests is one thing," he wrote, "and charging them with what as a rule they don't commit, is another." Lehmann as a "quondam Jew and professed infidel" had owned that he would enjoy the scandal, but Pen must *not* allow it. Perhaps Browning only wanted to strengthen his son's hand in the refusal Pen clearly intended to give, but the letter, with its insistence, reads as unnecessary nagging, since father and son agreed on what to do, although for different reasons.

Chapter Four

PAINTING AND SCULPTURE

One element in the wide scheme of his son's education had been more effective than Browning realised. Even when he was "cramming" for examinations, drawing lessons seem to have continued and country house visits afforded time and scope for practice. Millais once staying in the same house, they sketched together a group of fir trees. Millais was much impressed by Pen's work and suggested his entering on a career, the outcome of which has been—I think unfairly but almost universally—sneered at. He was not a genius and the period was a bad one, but some of the portraits of his father are surely excellent. There is merit too in the bust at Balliol, still more perhaps in his Dryope, and Rodin consented to take Pen for a while as pupil. "C'est étonnant," another French sculptor said of his rapid progress. His work suffered of course from the late start, but he threw his whole heart into it and worked so hard as to alarm Browning. It was now the father who urged rest and change on a son lodging above a butcher's shop in Antwerp and working feverishly under Jean-Arnould Heyermans, recommended by Millais as an outstandingly able teacher. In July 1875 Pen sent his father his own first composition—an old man gazing at a skull.

Hard as it is today to understand, impossible as it is to defend, Browning's treatment of this son of his, the depth of his affection can hardly be overstated. In the Isa letters, in Jowett's comments and those of all his intimates, we see it as the chief factor in these last two decades of his life. He wonders how long Pen will come in and kiss him good-night, he wonders how he will bear it when Pen has left him, even for the short university terms, he believes strangely enough that he knows how to "manage" the boy he so little understood—but this managing is entirely that of the loving parent whose duty it is to manage. This attitude of the period stands out in record after record, and those few of us who have lived through even its later years can never forget it. Authoritarianism was one aspect of parental love.

Pen had now the excuse of his art for long stays abroad, not only studying in Antwerp but joining a young group for summer months in the Black Forest, making his home a less and less frequented base. But his father quickly became useful with a new type of service. Beginning with his own house, then borrowing a larger area for Pen's huge canvasses from his good-natured publisher, George Smith, he gave a yearly exhibition of Pen's pictures. Letters are extant to Carlyle and other friends inviting them to see the paintings. And soon there were sales—not only, though perhaps primarily, to the father's friends and admirers. Pen won entry into European galleries, exhibiting in Paris and Brussels where a bronze of his was described as "empoignant ... grandement vu et éminemment sculptural." Some of his paintings even reached Australia. And of course the United States—although it must be admitted that one American purchaser at least was also one of the wealthy ladies perpetually vying for the poet's attention. It was rumoured that if not enough pictures found a purchaser, Browning put on a few stickers announcing them as sold.

But this was not all. There was much tiresome business to be done if the pictures were to appear on time in Paris, Brussels, or even further afield. Browning saw (with George Smith's assistance) that they were varnished when necessary, packed properly and shipped promptly. It all reminds one oddly of the husband who for many years had managed all practical matters for his unpractical (but also sick) wife. He asked Smith to ensure that Rodin should see his pupil's later work when visiting London, he asked him to get Millais's opinion, "which I prefer he should give you: it might seem suspicious in my mouth."

To Smith too Browning boasted of his son's new-found energy. He had "painted my portrait in four days—life size profile—certainly the best likeness ever taken of me." And again he had "painted eleven hours a day for the last two days. . . . Is not this good news?"

Pen is described as feeling later that his success had been due solely to his father's efforts. It was a pity that those efforts were—perhaps had to be—so obvious. But I doubt if even their love for Browning would have induced prominent British artists to give, as they did, public endorsement to what they believed inferior work. Jowett wrote "Your son seems to be making successful steps in his art, if I may judge from a criticism in the 'Maskod at

Antwerp' which I read this morning." He made too the pleasing comment: "There are few things better in this world than the round man being put in his round hole." Nor had Brussels or Paris judges any wish to please an English poet. But while Browning rejoiced in the sales, hoping too that they would help to build up the self-confidence Pen so notably lacked, he never realised that his own efforts might be instrumental in further diminishing it.

At one point London galleries became cautious for a comic reason. Browning's bitter attack on Horsley, the man responsible for refusing a picture of Pen's for the Royal Academy, may be read in his *Parleyings with Certain People of Importance in their Day.* Choosing a Florentine painter turned priest, described by his biographer as repenting for his pictures of naked women and ordering them burnt, "Nay *that* Furini, never I at least / Mean to believe," cries Browning. He goes on to attack Horsley under the name of his predecessor who had deplored the depicting of "God's best of beauteous and magnificent / Revealed to earth—the naked female form."

Horsley can hardly have enjoyed the description of himself under the guise of the repentant Florentine as "scruple-splitting, sickly-sensitive / Mild moral-monger." But, in rejecting the picture for the Academy, he had ensured also its rejection for the Grosvenor which had a rule of never taking Academy rejects. Browning coped with this after another fashion, calling at the gallery to make a personal entreaty. The tears coursing down his cheeks moved the authorities so much that they by-passed their own rule—thus giving Pen's picture an apparently special significance.

There is not material enough for, there would not be interest enough in, a full-size biography of Pen Browning, but there is, I think, enough to show him as a significant example of the effect of an adoring, unintelligent love combined with a sense of an authority little short of the divine with which parents felt themselves to be invested. Pen was beginning to escape from it—but was it too late an escape to be complete?

These years come to life in Browning's correspondence with Mrs. FitzGerald, edited by Edward C. McAleer with many illuminating notes. Within a few months of Pen's beginning had come his first success. "Three hundred pounds or guineas is a good round sum," wrote *The World*, "to get from a stranger for a first exhibited work, even if the young artist has had the rare sense not to exhibit until he knew how to paint; *and has had the good luck to be the son of a man and woman of genius.*" The italics are mine—for these words, although here kindly intentioned, were for Pen the sting in the tail so terribly frequent and so devastating for his self-confidence.

That summer he would not come to London but asked his father to see to the dispatch of the picture, adding "I shall do my best to have something for the Academy and Grosvenor." "Oh the blessed thing work is," commented Browning. The two pictures, neither representing naked women (which was a later Academy objection), were both placed. Mostly Pen worked at Antwerp, going to Paris for the Exposition that he might study the works there exhibited, writing very regularly ("His letters to me continue to be all that I could wish: He is clearly an artist born.... He is anxious to be back and at the brush again.")

Owing to Frederick Furnivall's insatiable curiosity we know something of a story the whole of which would be enlightening.

In 1877 Pen, now nearing thirty, was in Paris. He had continued, wisely enough, even though exhibiting, to go on working under his earlier masters. He is described on one at least of his pictures as "élève de M.M. J. P. Laurens et A. Rodin." M. Laurens had, it appears, in some way "crushed" his hopes. Pen was only too readily crushed. The lack of self-confidence is, as we have seen, often noted by his father, and Milsand, who was seeing him constantly, writes to Browning that he is "like a man who has been thrown two or three times from a housetop onto the pavement."

In this condition Pen's consolation lay in an attachment, or so Furnivall had heard, to the daughter of an innkeeper in Dinant. If this was a fact, it would be an interesting case of "up from the mill and back in three generations." Browning does not actually mention the father's profession—he rests his objection to the marriage mainly on the fact that Pen is still dependent on him and at the start of a career which ought at this stage totally to engage him. He remarks that the girl's parents are rich and goes on to say, "My objections were felt to be reasonable—I believe on both sides."

In Milsand's letters, which are the only contemporary evidence we have of Pen's state of mind, there is a mingling of deep sympathy with Pen and an unquestioning acceptance of a parent's rights. And we remember that Milsand himself postponed until his mother's death—a

Painting and Sculpture | 69

period of *ten years*—the marriage to which she was opposed. It was not in England only that parental authority was submitted to in a fantastic fashion.

Pen had evidently written very bitterly to his father and one hears an echo of his story many years later when "Michael Field" visited him at Asolo and decided that the father's behaviour was "a deep blot on his scutcheon." Maybe.

On the face of it one feels Pen should have accepted the challenge offered by his father's opposition. He was beginning to make *some* money from his pictures, and at that date very little English money would have been what was often called a "competence" had he decided to live in Belgium. Perhaps he knew that a competence was just what, without his father's help, he had never found adequate even for a bachelor. Perhaps the courage failed him to face again an angry father. Or of course the love involved may not have gone very deep. But was the upshot also another barrier to his full development?

He went on working, but by 1880 a letter from Browning seems to reveal an altered attitude: "he is always reticent, and never says more of a picture than that he hopes it turns out better than he expected." And again: "his reticence is such that I hear less than I like of his doings: and his habitual depreciation of them would mislead me were I not used to it." In 1880 the critics were "not good-natured to his picture," "Delivery to the Secular Arm," but Alma-Tadema had praised either that or some other work. "One such opinion," wrote Browning dismissing the critics scornfully, "is worth something." And galleries in London, Manchester and Melbourne were exhibiting him. In 1881 Browning wrote, "It is clear now that

Pen's preference is for a Continental life,—and as he thrives there,—thrives morally, I mean, in his love of work,—there is little good in wishing him transplanted." And in January 1882: "He has altogether proved a dear good considerate fellow during his stay here, and I feel it hard to part with him—even for his good as it promises to be."

In June 1883 comes the first mention of a ten-foot python from Senegal, which Pen was draping round his model while working on the statue of Dryope. The note on this states only that the model survived the snake, but according to another story this was only because Pen shot it when it began to tighten its coils dangerously.

A gold medal in 1883 and the exhibiting of his Dryope in 1884 are of course recorded, and in 1885 Browning, staying in Venice and joined there by Pen, speaks of him as blissfully happy both with the beauties of the city and the partial return to his childhood's surrounding. They discovered Ferdinando cooking for some friends. He loved Pen, he said, "come un figliolo" and exerted his utmost efforts to provide a fiesta for them both.

Browning fell in love with a house in Venice and entered into negotiations to buy it, realising that this would be the utmost he could do for his son's happiness. Pictures were selling, orders coming in and Pen had already rented a studio in Paris, where he had a picture on show, given, said Browning proudly, " 'a numéro'— that is a direction for adequate hanging—a distinction accorded him for the first time."

The purchase in Venice fell through, but on goes the story of Pen's achievements which one would dearly like to see from his side. Clearly he estimated his own work far less highly than did his father, but it is a teasing element in his story that only very few of his letters appear to be in existence. The destruction of this, and of other correspondences of far greater objective value, came about through Browning's change of residence. In 1887 he moved from Warwick Crescent to De Vere Gardens.

It was not long since the publication by Froude of Carlyle's cruel comments on so many of his friends had been widely condemned. Tennyson at that time had destroyed a good many letters, but he was far less savagely determined against public revelations of private matters than was Browning. The famous bibliophile (and forger) Thomas Wise has described his own anguish as, calling one day at Warwick Crescent, he watched letter after letter pitched into the fire, any one of which might contain matter, almost all bearing autographs, of worldwide interest. Browning's own letters to his family went of course—and equally no doubt his son's to him. This change of residence may well have caused a change of proportion in a picture none too easy to see clearly.

In the same year came Pen's engagement to Fannie Coddington, a young American heiress, to whom, he told his father, he had proposed unsuccessfully as long as fourteen years earlier.

Chapter Five

MARRIAGE

Browning was overjoyed, but characteristically his letters to Pen sketch a future designed by himself—a future which Pen had already tacitly rejected. They would of course have a house in London, Pen would of course pursue his career there under the happier conditions of domestic comfort provided by "dearest Fannie"—as she at once became. It was from Fannie's mouth that Browning received Pen's rejection of this scheme. Definitely they did not intend to live in England. But her reception as a daughter touched Fannie's heart. In a sketch of Browning written after his death, she spoke of it with deep feeling—and of Pen's likeness to his father as a decisive element in her acceptance of him. And she joined wholeheartedly in Pen's adoration of his dead mother, to whose memory a chapel was dedicated in their home. The marriage began happily, with a visit to Fannie's country—and the hopes of a baby which unfortunately miscarried. Soon came the purchase of the Palazzo Rezzonico in Venice. All this reaches us through Browning's comments, and the last also through comments by the outside world.

PEN BROWNING, CIRCA 1851

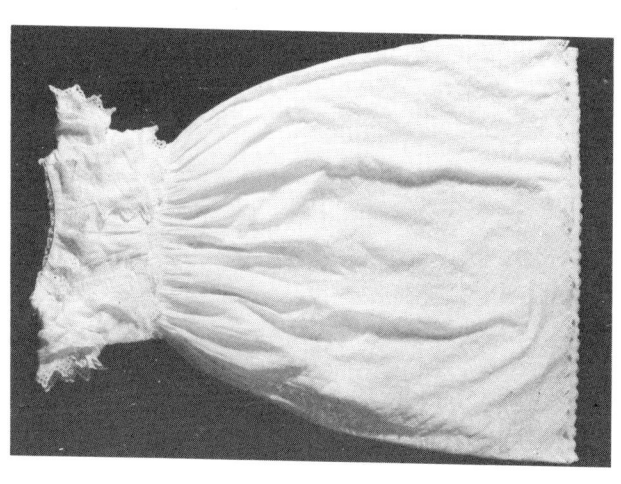

PEN'S CHRISTENING ROBE

PEN'S SKETCH OF HIS FATHER, 1853

CASA GUIDI

PEN BROWNING, 1858

PEN ON HORSEBACK, 1859
Oil by Hamilton Wild

PEN WITH HIS MOTHER, 1860

PEN BROWNING, 1862

PEN BROWNING, CIRCA 1864

PEN WITH HIS FATHER, CIRCA 1869

PEN WITH THE MILLAIS FAMILY IN SCOTLAND, CIRCA 1873

"THE ARTIST AT WORK"
Oil by J. Heyermans

PEN'S EXHIBITION MEDALS

"STILL-LIFE STUDY"
Water-colour by Pen Browning

"VESPERS"
Oil by Pen Browning

"THE MOONRISE"
Oil by Pen Browning

"THE COBBLER"
Oil by Pen Browning

"A WOMAN AT HER DEVOTIONS"
Oil by Pen Browning

"POMPILIA"
Bust by Pen Browning

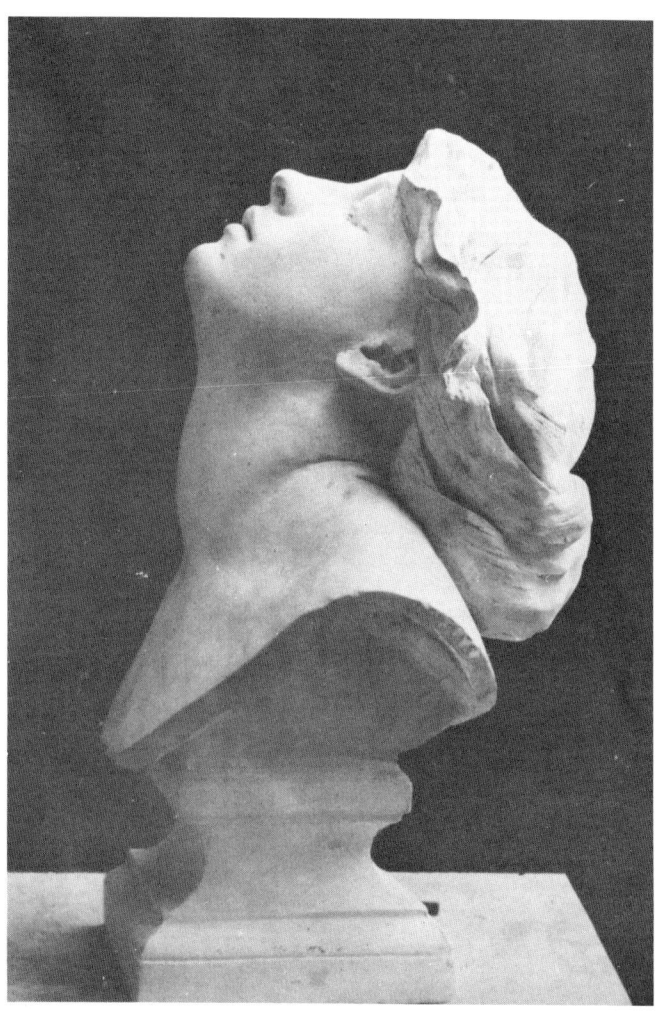

"HOPE"
Bust by Pen Browning

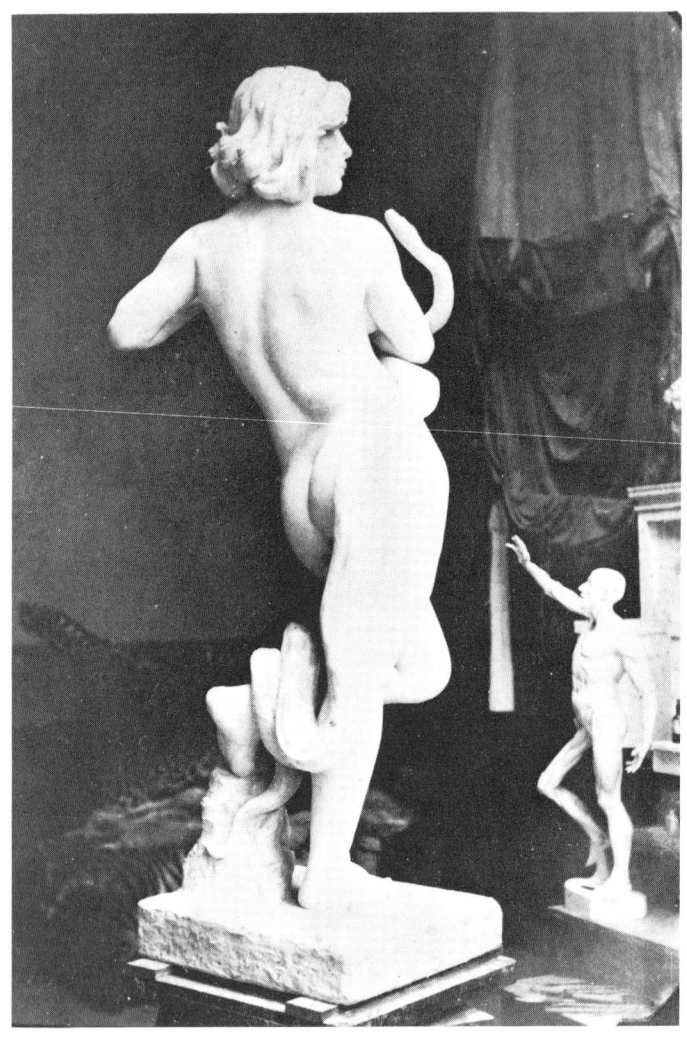

"DRYOPE"
Statue by Pen Browning

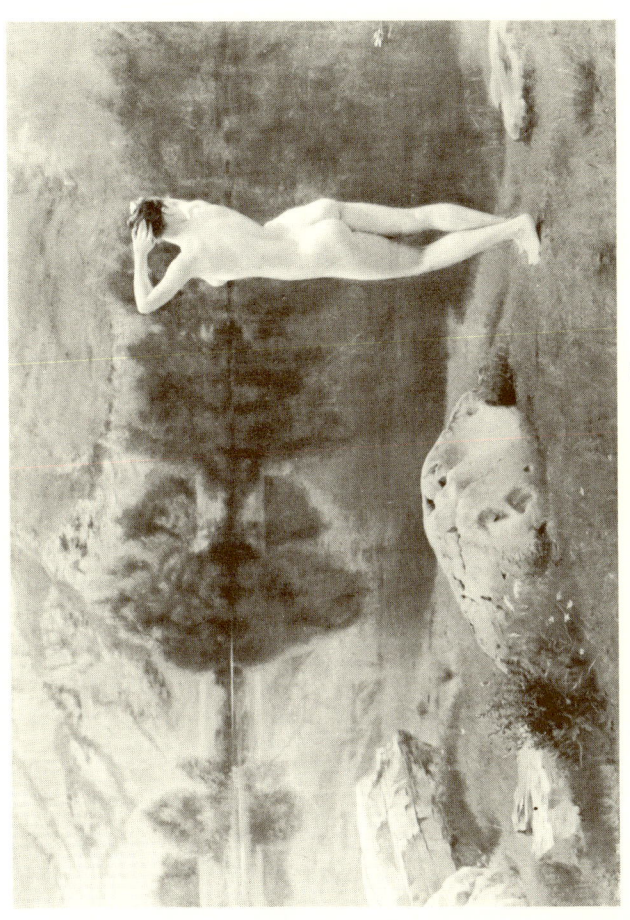

"NUDE STUDY"
Oil by Pen Browning

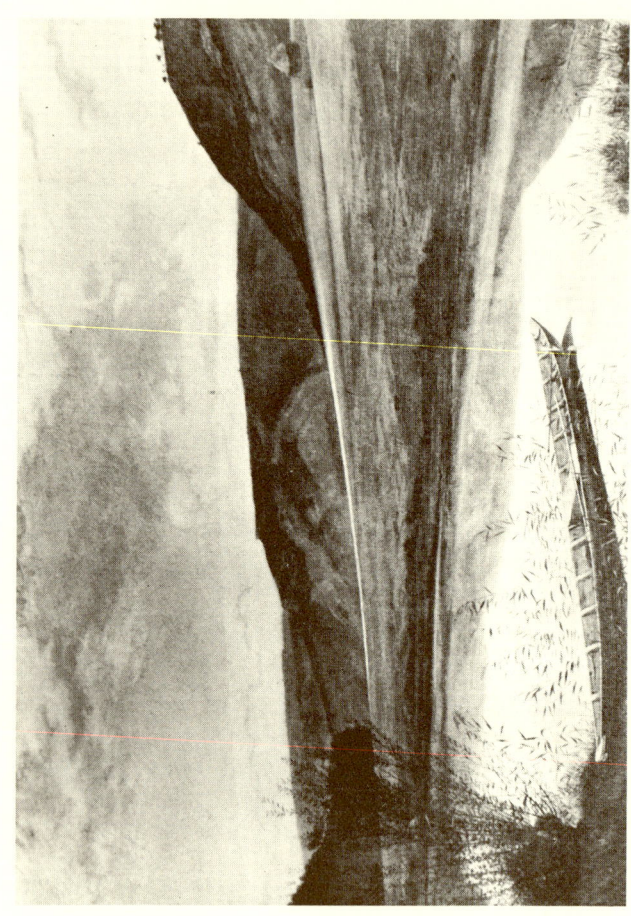

"DINANT ON THE MEUSE"
Oil by Pen Browning

"THE GLEANER"
Oil by Pen Browning

ROBERT BROWNING
Bust by Pen Browning

ROBERT BROWNING
Oil by Pen Browning

FANNIE CODDINGTON, 1872

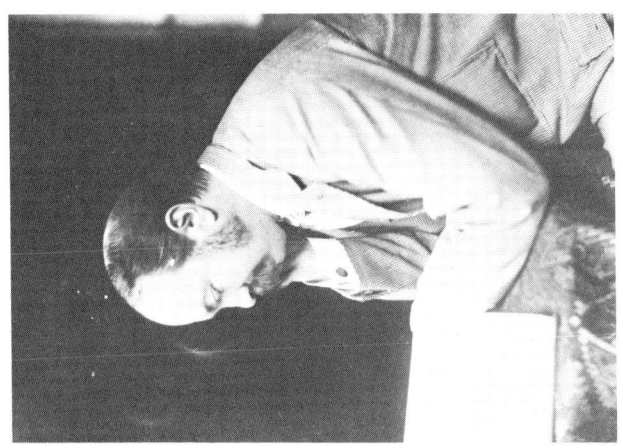

PEN BROWNING, CIRCA 1885

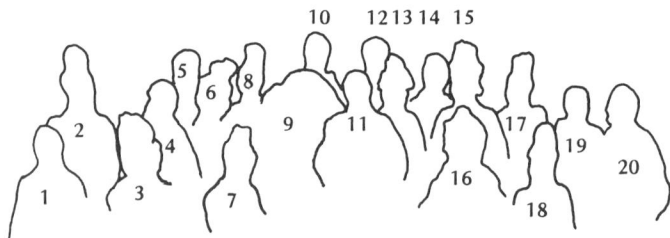

1. Arthur Schlesinger, later Berly
2. Mrs. Emilie Schlesinger
3. ?Miss Marie Coddington
4. Robert Browning
5. Unidentified
6. Miss Nora Berly
7. Miss Sarianna Browning
8. Unidentified
9. Fannie Coddington Browning
10. Unidentified
11. Pen Browning
12. Ernest Schlesinger, later Berly
13. Miss Emily Schlesinger, later Hawker
14. Henry Schlesinger
15. Miss Cornelia Berly, later Arbouin
16. Mrs. Berly
17. Unidentified
18. Miss Mary Schlesinger, later Talbot
19. ?Mr. E. L. S. Benzon, formerly Schlesinger
20. Unidentified

PEN'S WEDDING, OCTOBER 4th, 1887

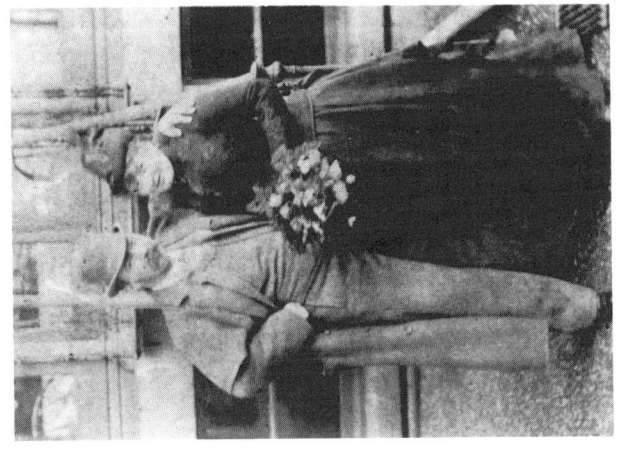

PEN AND FANNIE, CIRCA 1887

PALAZZO REZZONICO, 1890

PALAZZO REZZONICO, 1890

CARICATURE OF PEN

STREET SCENE AT ASOLO

PEN WITH HIS AUNT SARIANNA

PEN'S GRAVE AT ASOLO, JULY 8th, 1913

"What Pen Browning has done here," wrote Henry James, "transcends description for the beauty, and, as Ruskin would say, 'wisdom and rightness' of it. It is altogether royal and imperial—but Pen isn't kingly and the *train de vie* remains to be seen. Gondoliers ushering in friends from pensions won't fill it out." What did this mean—except perhaps that Henry James was the snob that he once feared his brother might call him? Pen's "train de vie" was indeed suspect from this point of view. His gondola was too magnificent: Freya Stark remembers the trailing draperies, the gorgeous gondoliers. Browning had allowed zealous friends to discover a pedigree for him, and get from the Heralds' College a coat-of-arms, but he did not make blatant use of it. Pen did. His gondoliers wore red tunics with wavy bands of gold and silver on their arms. None of this however could undo beauty, wisdom and rightness if these were indeed present in Pen's work on the Rezzonico. James comments a little later on Browning's pride in what he now calls Pen's "disproportionate palace," for "the mere supererogatory fixtures" of which dealers were unsuccessfully offering enormous sums.

Probably the "train de vie" had not satisfied James, but he continued to recognize Pen's genius in transforming a building. His father's utmost efforts could no longer spur him into painting or sculpture. Things already finished or near-finished were exhibited, but it was obvious that his energy was not so much tapering off as being otherwise directed. Loving care was put into the restoration of a Tiepolo ceiling at the Rezzonico, which was greatly admired by William Lyon Phelps. And Pen himself painted on canvas a vast scene for another ceiling. But Browning's exhortations and his entreaties for more original pictures or sculptures for exhibition went, we may be sure quite amiably, unheeded. For the most part his letters to Pen consist of a diary of his own doings which include the names of very many noteworthy people met day by day. Pen seems to have written to him often, Fannie almost every day.

It was a middle-aged marriage as age counted at that date, Pen being thirty-eight, Fannie a few years younger. Fannie's affection, one cannot but repeat, had reached the son by way of her admiration and love for the deeply devoted father, a father who must surely have exaggerated, to use a mild word, but whose *feeling* was sincere, when he wrote to Mrs. FitzGerald, "I would destroy every line I ever wrote if by so doing I could see fame and honour heaped on my Robert's head."

He thought too much of these honours. Pen had either despaired of them, on any really high level, or cared too little to exert himself in their pursuit. He was happy now in the transformation of his "disproportionate palace" and longing for his father's presence there. Quite possibly too Pen's eye troubles had already begun—the first reference I have found to them comes immediately after his father's death.

Browning came by way of Asolo on November 1st, 1889. He was of course in immediate request for parties, dinners, readings of his own poetry. Fannie Browning's little book conveys the weeks that followed far less vividly than the diary kept by her friend Evelyn Barclay. Evelyn tells of the poet's long readings—sometimes to the point of exhaustion, of the Rezzonico parrot for which he would save fruit, of his consideration for the servants who loved him dearly, of his insistence, even when coughing painfully, on keeping social engagements, of his contemptuous refusal of medical attention: "Doctors are all fools." The particular fools available were in consequence summoned too late.

Sarianna Browning wrote later that her brother had been in physical pain after the shock of reading the words, incredibly published by FitzGerald's biographer, in which he had expressed his "relief" at Mrs. Browning's death, going on to say, "No more Aurora Leighs thank God."

Browning was stirred into writing a verse which so appalled contemporary taste as to be for long omitted from his collected poems. Even Pen regretted it,—"Such words," he said, "recoil sufficiently on those who use them," and Browning was indeed persuaded to telegraph cancelling publication—a telegram the editor of the *Athenaeum* wisely did not open until the lines were actually in print.

> I chanced upon a new book yesterday: ...
>   —and learned thereby
> That you, FitzGerald, whom by ear and eye
>   She never knew, "thanked God my wife was dead."
> Ay, dead! and were yourself alive, good Fitz,
> How to return you thanks would task my wits.
>   Kicking you seems the common lot of curs—
> While more appropriate greeting lends you grace:
> Surely to spit there glorifies your face—
>   Spitting—from lips once sanctified by Hers.

The incident and its aftermath of self-defence (which included a correspondence with FitzGerald's friend

Tennyson) certainly contributed to the physical weakness and strain on the heart which became fatal after bronchitis had set in. Much more than the hackneyed final poem of *Asolando*, it is Browning's ultimate self-revelation. But his last thought as his heart began to fail was not of the adored wife whom he longed to meet again but of the son they had both loved so well and mishandled so badly. "I am dying. Oh my dear Boy, my dear Boy."

Probably as long as Browning lived the marriage of Pen and Fannie would have lasted despite the misfortune of one or more further miscarriages. In fact, their life together went on for a couple of years after Browning's death. It then simply ceased. Fannie at first lapsed into invalidism, bed and visits to health resorts, and then simply stayed away.

There had been one dangerous element from the first, the frequent presence of Fannie's sister Marie, imagined at first by Pen's father to be his choice. Her influence on Fannie had certainly been more than countered by that of Browning: daily letters, deep affection constantly emphasised on the one side, hero-worship on the other. And whatever Pen's "peculiarities," alluded to several times by Browning, his conviction had been that Fannie could cope with them. That the marriage was childless was a grief to them all and perhaps a determining factor.

Whether Fannie's ill-health was in part imaginary—Mrs. Miller gets from Henry James, who knew them both, that she modelled her "image" on that of her illustrious mother-in-law—the Rezzonico cannot have been an easy house to run or a comfortable one to live in. And both Wilson and Ferdinando were ageing. The Browning couple travelled and stayed in hotels, Wilson with them, apparently as Fannie's maid. Although she has been described as crazy, there seems no ground for this apart from Elizabeth's letters more than twenty years earlier in relation to a period of separation from Ferdinando and a surfeit of unguided Scripture reading. Clara Hahn, who when I met her was well into her nineties and hailed as the oldest contributor to the *Guardian*, told in that paper of meeting them at a mountain resort where Wilson skilfully contrived climbing trousers for her, using Pen's plus-fours as a pattern. Wilson, she told me, was reserved about Pen and Fannie, but talked incessantly of Pen's childhood—and of how his parents' over-indulgence had hampered her own efforts to prepare him for a responsible adult life.

A multitude of minor rather than any one major thing seems, as so often in such cases, to have led to the final breach between Pen and Fannie. Pen's snakes were naturally enough unacceptable to her; although certainly magnified in the stories she told, the presence of the most innocuous would be alarming to most women. There were too the birds greeting the dawn all too noisily. And then there was Ginevra.

Mabel Dodge Luhan, who came to know Pen after the separation but never (she says) heard a syllable from him on the subject, declares that Fannie brought Ginevra into the house as a sort of nurse-companion for herself. She was a magnificent creature—her son at Asolo showed me her photograph. And according to Mrs. Luhan, she posed for Pen until Fannie grew furiously jealous.

A more direct light is thrown on the story in an unpublished (and undated) letter from Katherine Wormeley to Dana Estes. She describes Ginevra as a model but says nothing of Pen in this connection. Fannie, she says, made a close friend of her, even introducing her socially. Obliged to go to England "under the care of a physician," she was determined to leave Ginevra in charge of the household in Venice. Sarianna begged her not to do this as it would most certainly anger the older servants. It was through one of them that Fannie's fears and jealousy were awakened. Anger came quickly to the boil soon after she reached England. Going on to America, she confided the story to her sister Marie, described here as an invalid. One wonders whether earlier letters showing Browning and Sarianna making considerable efforts to flatter and please this sister had indicated a tacit anxiety about possible danger. Anyway Marie "became very violent against Pen and is thought to be really the cause of Fannie's not listening to reason and allowing the matter to be cleared up and healed..."

But by now Pen's anger was also flaming. "He said to my people," continues Katherine Wormeley, "Do you suppose I would be such a villain as to insult my wife and aunt by making a girl in our very household my mistress?"

Anger, however, increased what Miss Wormeley calls "his characteristic defect... Pen is pig-headed to the last degree—obstinate as a mule." In his eyes, to send Ginevra away would be to blacken the character of "a girl Fannie had taken up and who had trusted Fannie in good faith."

All Pen's friends, she says, believe he is speaking the truth, although she herself is of opinion that Pen ought to have sent Ginevra away. But then she seems not to have known of the other rumour—that Ginevra was Pen's daughter! Her letter continues: "Fannie is wretched and longing to go back to him, but her sister stands in the way. Fannie says 'it will kill her if I do!'"

Nothing is more Victorian than this playing by an invalid, real or imaginary, on the sympathy of relatives. Nothing more commends Women's Liberation movements, even to women who feel themselves already quite happily liberated, than the ghastly picture of the "old maid" preying on those around her. Marie Coddington, despite her invalidism, carried on the fight with considerable spirit, stripping the Rezzonico of Fannie's furniture and keeping open by every means in her power the breach between husband and wife. "Had Mr. Browning lived," wrote Miss Wormeley, "it would not have lasted a day."

From Elaine Baly, great-grand-daughter of Robert Browning's Uncle Reuben, I heard something of Fannie's side of what was, like so much in Pen's life, a tragicomedy. Mrs. Baly's family memories go back to the beginning of the marriage, and she herself had known the woman who had been Fannie's companion for many years. In a letter to me she related what the companion had told her of Fannie's horror at Pen's nude sculptures—"so he posed the statues in the doorway, with drapery in front," but anyone entering the studio saw them as naked as Pen desired. The letter went on: "The supposed children by Breton girls were never discussed in the family in my hearing—however the name Ginevra cropped up many times, and Fannie's companion said that she was Pen's daughter."

Mrs. Baly showed me some fascinating pictures—including a photograph of a head sculptured by Pen, called "Hope," which might have been Ginevra. That she was Pen's daughter no one in her family doubts. But they are equally convinced that Pen was very much in love with Fannie. Photographs show her as too fat for modern taste but do not convey what Mrs. Baly describes as her chief beauties—glorious Titian red hair, lovely colouring, and sparkling eyes which lit up in moments of emotion. Pen, she says, loved to tease her, if only to awaken the animation brought by anger. He was "in love with her beauty and always wanted to show her off."

The wedding day itself had gone near to disaster. This cousin does not at all believe what is sometimes asserted—that Pen married Fannie largely for her money. Browning was indeed concerned about this for his very expensive son, but Pen was deeply in love. Yet love for his bride was not strong enough for neglect of his birds and animals even on his wedding day. He was so deeply concerned with their transportation that Fannie grew petulant and declared there would be no room left for her in the carriage. She had already become hysterical when offered a peacock feather pen to sign the register. Peacock feathers, she cried, were unlucky.

I had thought of Pen's extravagance as the main cause for the final disruption of the marriage, but Mrs. Baly disagrees. Fannie, she says, was very rich and overwhelmingly generous. Venetian gossip confirms this—saying that her gifts to strange foreign missions irritated Pen. The poverty at the end of Fannie's life was, says this Browning relative, the result of fantastic lawsuits in which she would hire one lawyer after another. Certainly what the law can cost has proved for many a bottomless pit.

The marriage, even if badly strained, did go on for two years after Browning's death. A letter from his aunt Sarianna to Anne Thackeray (Lady Ritchie) in October 1891 says they are both joining her in Florence, having been taking cures at two different spas. Elaine Baly has a guide-book inscribed by Pen: "Fannie from her R.B.B. on their first visit here together (Florence Oct. 22 1891.)" Turning the pages one sees pictures and statues marked for special attention and on each day a note of whether they had gone alone or been accompanied by aunt Sarianna or by Mr. and Mrs. Story.

Mrs. Baly had heard nothing of the tale told by Mrs. Luhan of Pen's love for Edith Story. This does not prove it untrue—what anyone hears of anything is largely a matter of chance. But Pen's faithfulness to old friends is a strong point in his character. That he saw Edith often is certain, and that he helped her financially when her son got deep in debt. And she was with him when he died. But was the relationship one of passion or the resumption of what had been an elder sister's affection warmly returned by a five-year-younger brother? What is certain is that it belonged to Pen's long-lasting but now long lost and very happy childhood for which nostalgia persisted.

Fannie too had memories—of six brothers all dying in childhood and six sisters one of whom remained terribly alive if not always beneficent.*

It is not easy to separate the grain from the chaff in the mass of rumour and conjecture surrounding the famous dead—but how much more difficult with the relatively unknown! There are at Baylor University many letters, some of them making the strangest assertions, some warning their recipients how unreliable these other informants are. And researchers have left statements of extreme improbability with no evidence offered—as that Eleanora Duse, the great Italian actress, wished to be buried near Pen, thus starting a scandal and causing Fannie to move his body. Or of an earlier date—that Pen had *on their wedding day* told Fannie of his illegitimate child by another woman and asked her for money to send them! This story comes we are told from a Mr. Grove who had "no use for Pen." But whether or not Pen told Fannie of this on the wedding day, or later, or at all, I have recently had a letter which suggests that he did in fact have a son born within a year or so of the marriage. The letter is from Cecil Barrett Browning who calls Pen his grandfather and mentions that his own father, Pen's son, died in 1958 aged 69. The letter gives no further details, and my request to Cecil Barrett Browning for further information came back to me through the Dead Letter Office.

*Thomas Butler Coddington (1814-86) married Almira Flaxton Price (1819-78) on October 17th 1837. Their children were: Martha Ann (1839-75); John Delion (1841-47); Thomas Moore (1842-47); Fredrick Meyer (1844-47); Maria and Louise, twins, (1845); Charles Theodore (1847); William Mumford (1848-51); Emily (1849-1924); David FitzRandolph (1851-55); Fannie (September 6th, 1853 - September 20th, 1935); Marie Frederika (1856-1929); and Louisa (1858-59).

To return to the man who "had no use for Pen": he asserted that Pen never finished his own pictures, that he had lived for seven years with the innkeeper's daughter at Dinant who became the mother of the child that Pen asked Fannie to pay for; that he and Fannie had never slept together (in which case by whom was Fannie supposed to have miscarried?); that she had really wanted to marry his father, who had "forced" Pen to marry her. But thus grows rumour and, if hard to sort out with the famous, Pen was a man so little known as to make refutation (or confirmation) difficult if not impossible.

Much of this rumour had been heard by Lilian Whiting, a warm friend of both Pen and Fannie, who wrote a book about Pen's parents, which, though sometimes lacking in accuracy, has much in it that is worthwhile. She is, it is true, a gusher, very much out of tune with the present day, or indeed with scholarship of any date, but with a close personal knowledge and (more unusually) a warm affection for both husband and wife. On a long evening with Fannie she heard *her* story of the marriage; from her own affectionate understanding of Pen she conjectured his. Conjectured, yes, for as Mrs. Luhan has stated, Pen did not talk.

Lilian Whiting's insights are I think of real value. She was perplexed and unhappy over a situation which she recognised as inevitable, but she saw qualities in both husband and wife which made it singularly painful. Her judgment is that Fannie's upbringing had been of that narrow fundamentally unchristian quality which claimed in the nineteenth century to represent Christianity. That she was in consequence of it in dire need of psychological treatment. That this, rather than any physical illness, was what drove her from doctor to doctor to the end of life. Yet Lilian had a very real affection for Fannie, who one evening had begged her to stay while she poured out her story.

Fannie long outlived her husband, and in 1921 Lilian Whiting wrote to Dr. Armstrong of Baylor University, who was trying to get into touch with her. He apparently had felt snubbed and baffled. Writing to advise him, she dwells on the unfortunate results of Fannie's upbringing in a world so well known to her and puts forward her conviction that the misfortune of total misfit rather than any fault had wrecked their marriage. "... I have the impression" she wrote on April 25th, 1921, "that if you should totally ignore any lapse on Mrs. Barrett Browning's part and should write her, regarding a call, as if nothing had occurred, that she would receive it and respond in the same spirit.... The spiritual tragedy of that marriage! Barrett Browning was simply formed and fashioned of the loveliest elements; he was simply adorable; and she not without unusual quality; yet these two people apparently only brought out each other's worst, all the time. And yet ... his divine patience with her ... well ... one cannot go into all that now...."

Twenty years later (August 1941) she was writing again, emphasizing more strongly the same view. She had heard from Edith Peruzzi of a dinner at the Rezzonico when "Pen was in happiest spirits and Fannie was charming." Suddenly however she left the room, and they heard her from upstairs apparently lying kicking on the floor. In vain both went up "and entreated." She had locked the door and would not open it.

Marriage | 117

One might suspect this story as highly coloured by Edith Peruzzi—but Sarianna Browning too has written of "Fannie's *fits* of hysteria, screaming and crying, one could hear her down the street."

Mrs. Whiting calls it a mysterious and "torturing disease." Sarianna declared that Pen should have been warned of it before the marriage.

Mrs. Luhan is best known from her long friendship with D. H. Lawrence. But she has written voluminously also about her memories of friends in both the old and new world, devoting several pages to Pen, for whom she had a sincere affection and indeed a good deal of admiration. Her prejudice against Fannie is undeniable, but she mentions no meeting with her.

All Mrs. Luhan's memories come to us on a high note of drama, and it is anyone's choice how far to trust her accuracy when she relates the stories which she declares Fannie was telling of her husband—all over Europe— "that he was a pervert, he was degenerate, he kept mistresses in the same house with her . . . large snakes in the basement." She herself (she said) never mentioned him to anyone without horrified reaction: "What, *that* man!"

One snake at least was, as we have seen, factual although not poisonous. But it was not snakes, birds or sexual aberrations even, that brought about the break. However generous about money Fannie may have been, Pen's extravagance must have got on her nerves. His own fortune was very small up to the death of his father, his expenditure was never small at any date. For months twenty workmen at least were employed on renovation and improvement of the Rezzonico; the vast building was made more comfortable by central heating. Two gondoliers stood at the ready at its front door.

Letters from Henry James to Mrs. Bronson, however, suggest much worse things than extravagance. He had dragged in the dust, says James, the two honoured names of his parents. Exactly how is not explained, but it is clear enough that James and the group with whom he consorted in Venice accepted pretty much everything Fannie—or rumour—told them.

According to Mrs. Luhan, one excellent reason for this was that Pen never put forward his own side of the story. When told of the version circulating, says Mrs. Luhan, "all over Europe," as Fannie moved from one boarding house to another, he "looked deprecating and a little more puzzled than usual," but he refrained from retort "even with us whom he came to know so well." Such silence in a not too generous world seems to have done him harm. Nor need rumour have spelt precisely what Fannie was saying. Stories can spring up from nowhere, growing as they pass from group to group. A shrug or a tear may soon become a full grown story of cruelty.

Besides his surely remarkable reticence, one notes in Pen a striking faithfulness to old friends. He had as we have seen taken into the Rezzonico both Ferdinando and Wilson. He had also when his father died taken his aunt Sarianna to live with him—which she did till her death at the age of eighty-four.

The fact of the modelling, whether of Ginevra or/and his snakes, shows that Pen was still working as an artist up to or near the time of the separation. But his extraordinary skill with buildings continued to develop—and at a date I cannot exactly determine, his sight had begun to make painting a problem.

There had been in the Rezzonico a chapel to his mother's memory, but when that Venetian palace was sold Pen bought the Casa Guidi, in which he stored the relics of both parents.

It was in Florence that Mabel Dodge Luhan knew him. She paints a vivid picture, especially of his relationship with Edith Story, who had become Countess Peruzzi—one of the titles created by the ruling house and despised by an aristocracy dating back to the early middle ages. Edith, according to Mrs. Luhan, had hated the intellectual, artistic world of her parents and was determined to get away from it. She was now growing old, was very fat and plain, but above all very unhappy. Her deeply loved son Bindo had been cashiered from the Italian army for homosexuality. He had appeared set for a brilliant career, handsome, graceful and popular, but of all his old friends almost all had abandoned him. He lived in the same house as his mother, on another floor, and whenever Pen came to see her she would ask him to look in on Bindo—something, says Mrs. Luhan, which represented social suicide for any man. But Pen always did it.

He was, she says, in love with Edith, who for her part cared only for Bindo. Whether this is true is a question almost impossible to answer; Mrs. Luhan is not always accurate. And Pen's faithfulness to old friends, noted in relation to Wilson, Ferdinando and his aunt, would have extended to Edith and her family. She, too, was part of his real life—that childhood life in Italy. Certainly he saw her often, and with both her sons she visited him at the Antella.

One of the wildly improbable rumours I was told was that Pen was Bindo's father. Mrs. Luhan, picker-up of gossip though she was, had clearly heard nothing of this—and appearances were certainly against it.

Bindo was the incarnation of grace and beauty, Pen plump and red-faced, "looking just like an apple." But when she adds that Pen was extraordinarily stiff, she must surely be wrong about the athlete of earlier years and the man who could still drive not only a pair of horses in tandem but, according to the engineer Cantoni of Asolo, five horses together.

It seemed amusing to his Barrett cousins to call him "Cochon" and a rather clever cartoon has survived in which the body of a pig has Pen's face. But it cannot have been amusing for Pen.

He dressed usually in checks, giving something of the impression of an English country squire, but he confided in Mrs. Luhan that he never made a new acquaintance without noticing the start, the astonished question asked not in words but by looks: "What, *that* the son of two poets!"

Chapter Six

DOING HIS OWN THING

Lilian Whiting's sense of inevitable tragedy in Pen's marriage permeates also an account given by another American, Julia Schelling, who admired Fannie immensely, noting her charity to slum children in New York, her interest in missionary activities and her personal piety. Yet she came to feel that Fannie's dominant personality, the spirit of her Dutch Protestant ancestry, coupled with a deep and sincere religious fervour, contrasting strongly with the easy Bohemian character of her artist husband, was a chief cause for estrangement. "Her outlook on life was a very narrow one; his almost too broad."

She tells more than Lilian Whiting of the efforts at reconciliation, describing how, after the Rezzonico had been closed and Pen had gone to Alexandria (where some Browning relatives were living), Fannie was persuaded to join him there.

In his *Reminiscences* A. H. Sayce records that on his way from Egypt he was invited by Pen to lunch at the Rezzonico: "There had been a reconciliation between him and his wife, and she had arrived in Venice a few days previously, and he wished to introduce me to her.

I had been in the drawing room a few minutes only when I heard a hysterical shriek which rang through the whole building, and Browning entered the room shortly afterwards in a state of agitation. He told me that his wife had been seized with a sudden fit of illness. She left Venice the next day and, I believe, never saw her husband again."

Can this hysteria have followed Pen's revelation that he was publishing his parents' love letters? For Julia Schelling gives this as a reason for their separation unnoted by other commentators. So passionate was Fannie's feeling, that when Julia acknowledged that she had not read them, Fannie cried "I love you for that. I have never read them myself. They are too sacred for even my eyes to look upon."

Despite her realization of Fannie's limitations, Julia's sympathy had been totally with her, and she describes sadly the "insolent custom officials" when Fannie despatched her belongings to America. For they "like all Venice resented her desertion."

But later Julia visited Asolo and although not losing her sympathy with Fannie came away with a very different outlook on Pen. For there she discovered a work in which, refusing to "commercialise" it, Pen was enabling the women and children of Asolo to live on a higher level. He had opened a school of linen weaving and lace making, using on the linen an outline of the castle as a trade mark, selling the goods at the Rezzonico and investing the proceeds towards further development.

> I was amazed to find no building or structure of any kind. There was only an open field with arbors

of grape vines reaching from one end to the other. There were upwards of a hundred girls and women seated on wooden benches with little cushions and spindles on their laps weaving the intricate designs that Barrett Browning had taken from works of art, or weaving with hand looms beautiful raw silk into useful articles. The happy faces of these workers, the bright sunshine, the fresh air, and the exquisitely artistic work filled us with wonder. I know of no other memorial that, while creating something beautiful, also brings health and happiness to so many workers.

Pen called at the hotel where Miss Schelling and a group of young friends were dining and took them to visit the castle, where she was greatly impressed by a statue of his—Eve, with the face of "the beautiful model whom I had met in Venice." But total disapproval is heard no longer in her voice as Pen "filling our hands with roses and our hearts with happy memories," she and her companions "sped into the night, never again to hear the soft English voice of our charming host, never again to judge too harshly the son of Elizabeth and Robert Browning."*

Two other visits are fully described in memoirs of the period—one, in 1895, coming from the minor poets mentioned earlier who called themselves jointly Michael Field, the other in 1904 from William Lyon Phelps.

Asolo and the Brownings, by Julia E. Schelling. The hundred girls at work on the lace is a much higher figure than that given by other observers. It may have gone up and down according to the sales.

The aunt and niece have given perhaps the best picture of Pen's life at Asolo and of the atmosphere of what was then a lovely, isolated and self-contained village city.

"... The healing greatness of nature draws close to our carriage. Lovely peasant girls look at us—we even hear the sound of runlets ... chestnuts and acacias and oaks are green above the greenest grass ... There is La Rocca —the timeless fortress, and that cluster of houses below is Asolo.

"At the inn—Pen steps up to our window—he greets us with the generous courtesy and the very tone of voice we loved in his father."

Even before showing them their rooms at the inn and taking them on to tea at what he called the "Palazzo Pigstye," Pen rushed into an account of his efforts to prevent a duel between a young Italian count and an Englishman whose name would be known to them both. Aunt and niece are hungry and tired. But they must go round by the lace school, so central in Pen's thoughts, where they will find Sarianna—and it seems a long walk before they reach the Casa Browning—past the house where *Asolando* was written, past the market place "with the chestnuts on a little hill above the fountain ... the weedy loveliness of Catherine Cornaro's castle ... the ferny walls that bound the Riva."

They only counted five dogs which rushed out barking to meet them. There were we know at least seven, but their tumult was drowned by the birds whose "full moment" came as tea was served on the lawn. "Peacocks screech, the macaws shriek, doves come in with their cotton-wool sounds, geese chatter, the hounds bay—chickens faintly fluster, turkeys puff out their cheeks—

I say in a word it is as if Noah's ark had landed on the Casa Browning slopes, and all the living creatures been turned out thereon."

Again we feel the link between child and man—for at seven years old Pen had loved his rabbits as today he loved his birds and dogs. His mother had copied with pride:

My Rabbits *(seven years old.)*

1

My rabbits are pretty and pretty—
They are white, with pink-painted eyes.
On the outside all a fluffy white,
To make their coats so warm.
I used to take them with my arms,
And kiss them with my love!
I could not catch them till they liked,
They ran like little hares—
I gave them all the sweetest apples
That were growing in the world.

2

I could not bear my eyes upon
The pussy walking in the yard—
Because I feared, because I feared
That he would jump upon the wall,
And eat my little rabbits.
But *I* was standing on the terrace,
As well as he upon the wall;
And I began to raise my voice
And sing, 'O pretty little pussy,

'In your day-dress, in your day-dress!
'Are you going to wear a day-dress
'To come here to my wedding fair
'Of my pretty rabbits?'

3

But the pussy said, 'Goodbye!
'For I'm going to *my* wedding,
'And *you* are going to *yours*!
'And I'll give my wedding-ring
'To my little kittens;
'And you'll give your wedding-ring
'To your little rabbits!
'And I wish you a good wedding;
'And I wish you a golden ring,
'Which shall be always Your's!'

Even inside the house, full though it is of "old chests and chairs and bronzes," the birds dominate—peacock feathers and sunshine in the Sala d'Ingresso and the tiny drawing room "enlivened chiefly by a couple of plumes from those magnificent cockatoos on the terrace."

They stayed from May 21st to June 9th, 1895, paid a more lengthy visit to the lace factory and bought some of the beautiful patterns. "Here were the bambini working on their lace pillows where Pippa wound her silk. Curious to think that our poet is as much at the bottom of this charming industry as of *Asolando* . . . these little people clicking their bobbins at their blue tables in the airy upper chamber, are there because he has lived and loved Asolo."

Surely this is a supreme instance of the son's problem in "doing his own thing" under his father's shadow! Yet to a point he wished and had chosen it; he had dedicated this creation of his own to his father's memory.

The eve of Whitsunday they find at the Palazzo "heaps and heaps of letters on the floor (such curious things of Robert's, Sarianna says—his copy of Shelley as a boy —the proof sheets of *Paracelsus*, inscribed to his mother, etc.)" The Shelley shown to them is the one so graphically described by Frederick Pottle in *Browning and Shelley: A Myth and Some Facts*. And they felt that it was strange Sarianna did not see that the volume was *theirs* as simply as a wedding ring belonging to a woman. "Every scribbling was alive to us, but the 'rare thing' vanished from our sight—to be bequeathed to whom?"*

Pen talks of the Tuscan climate and the problems it sets for the painter, all the changes being "short as seconds; evening is exquisite and over before the brush can fix it—just an instant when things float and have golden haloes and it is night."

They feel him on this subject very much "the son of two poets" describing "the blank walls so characteristic, like some strong unamicable trait in a friend—the touch of rose or oleander connecting them with the sky, the fret of olive shadows on them, and below them dust, inches deep as snow is."

They feel Pen to be "most touching in his sensitiveness and humility. He says he is a failure, and yet he has the artist's temperament and a delicacy that is finely touched. The amount of misunderstanding he has met with and his own sorry sense of his personal deficiencies

*This volume is in the Robert H. Taylor Collection, Princeton, N. J.

has driven the poets' son deep within the shell of Barrett commonplaceness.... His eyes are still his mother's—ardour and timidity almost war in them—yet they are lost under fat brows tortured with rheumatism. He has his father's seriousness, thinks about life till he is on the road to madness, and escapes with jocund instinctive habits of life, like those of a squire ... has an irritable temperament and a patient heart ... is very proud and therefore suffers internally ... his high birth from poets makes him nervous; his personal humility brings as it always does patience."

Not always are the moods of these two ladies so sympathetic. Early in the visit Sarianna had been "Dear old Miss Browning" and Pen "a thoroughly good fellow," indeed the family (apparently including Ginevra in house and lace factory) "entirely human and kind." But as the visit drew to its close Pen's going off for a ride, forgetful that he has promised to take them to the Torricella is "somewhat chilling." Moreover "somehow Sarianna's unloveableness weighs on us now we must part with her"—in fact "it is useless to think that the Brownings will act gracefully; they sometimes speak so, but are far too absent and self-absorbed to carry out their words. Even our poet was no exception."

In short, they had been in Asolo too long; reaction had set in. Yet a number of letters from Sarianna followed the visit, and show that the friendship persisted however chequered by moods. We learn that when the crops were bad Pen was on a committee for the relief of poverty. "He has already got the name 'Cuccina Economica' to be changed to 'Cuccina Popolare;' the former suggests something cheap and bad—he is really anxious that the soup should be strong and nourishing, that the idea of charity should be got rid of, and the hardworking poor should look on it as a privilege to be able to buy 'superior food at a low price.' "

The next year Pen, still in possession of the Rezzonico. lent it to the municipality of Venice for a "Grand Charity Ball for the Croce Rosa . . . It was the most magnificent fete given in Venice for more than a century, and they realised about 17,000 francs. At the beginning of the year Pen was made Cavaliere of the Corona d'Italia."

Visiting some American friends, Mr. and Mrs. Walter F. Brown of Providence, R.I., in Venice, Pen told them triumphantly, "You will be glad to know that I have at last paid back Fannie the whole sum she put into the restoration."

Besides his dwelling in Asolo Pen had bought the Torre all'Antella, where he was sought out in 1904 by William Lyon Phelps. He had personally restored it, replacing loosened stones and discovering every detail whereby to bring back its trecento character and beauty.

Phelps seems to have cared little about this: he notes the screeching birds held in Pen's hands to the great peril of his eyes, but what *he* wanted was what almost everyone else did, one detail after another about Pen's father. He got some interesting answers—and learnt too that his host still felt himself to be an Englishman. Pen also lamented the time wasted on his own musical education—and declared that he played much better than his father, who was practising five-finger exercises to the end of his life! Pen's attitude to his father was ambivalent— he at once loved and admired and was irritated by him.

His adored mother he could never have discussed. Showing a friend one day the manuscript of *Aurora Leigh*, he mentioned (as we learn from Lilian Whiting) that after his death it would go to the Bodleian at Oxford. The friend suggested he should give it now when he could see that it was properly placed. His answer was, "No, I could never part with it while I live."

Phelps describes "a smart pair of horses hitched tandem," which "carried us along at high speed; they were spirited and skittish, but were beautifully handled by my host."

The description of Pen's appearance he gives is an echo of Mrs. Luhan's: "A short man, like his father, rotund and red-faced and the red veins traced patterns on his cheeks and brow."

William Lyon Phelps was not, as Mabel Luhan became, an intimate friend, but finding some of Pen's pictures interesting, he felt that he "might have achieved a high reputation if he had not carried the burden of his parents' fame." It is interesting to contrast this and similar interviews with Henry James's view, derived from stories told him by Americans settled in Venice, of Pen dragging the names of those parents in the dust. Yet Pen, besides collecting every relic of them both and enshrining them first at the Rezzonico and then at the Casa Guidi, kept alive their memory to a degree that few sons of the famous have approached.

He defended to Phelps the recent publication of their love letters, received with a storm of anger by many besides Fannie and the Barrett clan. It had probably been urged on him by George Smith—no man to lose a best-seller through any squeamishness, a close friend of Browning's, asked by him to guide and help the middle-aged man of whom his father could never think as other than a boy.

It was of course the unpleasing picture the Barretts disliked of their very unpleasing grandfather, but it is certainly debatable whether in terms of the nineteenth century still dragging on into the twentieth it was too soon for that fascinating book. Pen's defence was at least plausible—had he left it to others it might have been edited and cut: his father, destroying almost the whole of his correspondence, had saved these precious letters and left them for him to deal with. Should he destroy or leave to others what had been put into his hands? One day he would, he believed, be justified—and Phelps asks whether perhaps that day had already come.

Very different was the opinion of the Barrett family. From Jamaica C. J. Moulton-Barrett wrote to the *Standard* of a "lack of delicacy hardly conceivable" shown by Pen's publication. "His mother would have been horrified. She loved her father." The letter goes on to state in defence of that father the very facts that had driven Robert and Elizabeth into their long-considered action. "My sister had been an invalid for years. By the direction of Dr. Chambers her room was kept at a certain temperature, and she never left it . . .

"Under these circumstances my father lost his daughter . . . He never recovered from it . . . few fathers would have taken the hand of a man who had so acted . . . few sons, either for gain or love of notoriety, would make public the confidential letters of their mother."

What can Pen have felt as he read this and much more of a long abusive letter? Surely a deep reassurance lit by a few cynical smiles. His mother's restored health and fifteen years of a life that can only be called blissful, his own existence too, can scarcely have seemed negligible even if there had been nothing else to weight the scales against a father whose excuse for his oppression could only be that of an unbalanced mind. I doubt whether this letter disturbed at all the tranquility one senses growing in Pen Browning as tranquil Asolo became increasingly his home.

Mrs. Bronson had been a very dear friend of Browning's and for his sake she was kind to Pen. One of his rare letters indicates a probably passing misunderstanding—but she seems to have seen him often when they were both in Asolo. The link of their love for pets is shown in a Valentine he addressed to her dog, which was pleasantly named "Contenta."

> How could you be Contenta if you were not content?
> Things being as they are there's little to lament,
> But if instead of being man I were of race canine
> I'd ask you for your pretty paw to be my Valentine.

It was at Mrs. Bronson's house, La Mura, in Asolo that Henry James had been staying when he became half aware as early as 1899 that a new day had dawned for Pen Browning.

Half aware? Yes. For he did not realize that there was more in what Pen was doing than the mere "self-aggrandizement" of ownership. James wrote, visiting Mrs. Bronson

> Pen was there to dinner 2 of the nights—and showed me all his wondrous property including the boa-constrictor, the new mountain (he *has* literally

bought one) and the husband of Ginevra. He did not speak of his (own) wife, but seemed in gayish spirits—and I had a strange lurid vision of the *fond* of all his conduct. . . . Roughly speaking, it is vanity and pride of possession and proprietorship—the *owning* (the air and grandeur of it) of half that little place; the being, there, the great swell. There! —Fancy playing to *that* gallery. It's wonderful what he owns—and what he has done with it. His talents in this line [are] great. And his box at the theatre. He's the Asolan Kaiser Wilhelm. There's nothing over for Fannie. The Torricella is a marvel. It makes me realize what he is anchored to. Basta.

As with his sport and his painting, Pen Browning was out of due time with his other talent acclaimed so fervently by Henry James. Nobody is going to bother overmuch about whether the restoration of the Rezzonico or the Torre all'Antella is correctly done as they do about the barbarism of the Notre Dame restorations, and indeed we hardly know today what was done by Pen and what by later owners. But James was no fool, and we can I think assume that where he saw near-genius there was at least remarkable talent.

Exactly what he had heard when he wrote earlier of the honoured names Pen had *dis*honoured, we shall probably never know. But about Asolo we can learn a good deal which, while partly confirming his account, shows Pen's actions in a very different light.

Browning the poet had been content with an idyllic picture of Pippa the bare-footed, singing child, her one-day holiday, and the power of her goodness on other human lives. Pen seems to have seen in one aspect far more deeply. The old old woman whom I met in Florence remembered his taking from heavy field work a frail young girl and bringing her into his household as a maid. She scouted the notion of sexual attraction—and Pen was by then on in years. It was, she said, sheer compassion. As a tribute to his father he had first considered reviving what had inspired Browning to write *Pippa Passes*. He had bought the now crumbling tower where Pippa had worked, but the silk industry of those days being dead, he employed the girls as we have seen at two other skills: the lovely Venetian lace in old patterns, and, the hand-woven linen were bringing to Asolo a new prosperity. Pen's former model, Ginevra—more recently house-keeper for himself and his aunt Sarianna—was put in charge. She had married his "Intendant" with whose son, "Engineer" Cantoni (both these words seemed to be used as titles), I had (with the aid of an Italian dictionary) a long and on his side an animated conversation.

Chapter Seven

AS PEN IS STILL REMEMBERED

The young Cantoni, now grown old, remembered Pen from his boyhood—the five horses, harnessed together in various formations, the immense wealth (this was repeated everywhere in Asolo) the kindness to him and other children.

That great traveller, Freya Stark, driven to a house on the hillside by the hideous traffic today ruining the little town, remembers the splendour of his gondola and gondoliers lent to her parents for a holiday to be spent at the Rezzonico, and a day when he lunched with them in Asolo:

> ...and cut an orange into human shape with eyes and legs and arms made of thin strips of peel, and a mouth somewhere about the equator. He puzzled me by saying, as he handed this object to me, that it was his portrait, and I can now hardly distinguish, in my childish memory, the likeness from the original, except that Pen wore a hard straw boater on top of his general roundness. He was a sculptor of ugly gigantic figures, and he might have written poetry if two distinguished poets had not been his

parents, but his true gift lay in his restoring and re-adapting of old houses, which he would transform into things of beauty—and then abandon.

No-one has conveyed better than Freya Stark the nostalgia one senses in all those who lived in Asolo as once it was and as it comes back to her "a symbol of happiness even now."

> The country around Venice is full of baroque or renaissance villas falling into decay: Pen bought and restored three of these in Asolo, a tiny but complete city forty miles from Venice, laid out in the lap of a hill under the shell of a cruiser-shaped pre-Roman fortress. Below it is a little square with trees, and a fountain that spouts from under the pedestal of a fat lion sitting on its haunches. On a low spur opposite is the castle Tower of Catherine Cornaro, last Queen of Cyprus, who kept a gay provincial court here when Venice had brought her from her island. It is a sleepy little town, well away from railways and main roads. Its streets are lined with crooked porticoes, irregular and at uneven heights above the road, each house having decided for itself the shape and altitude of arches it liked best; and most are white-washed although a few painted façades remain with thin but splendid colours. Two ragged walls descending from the fort cut off a segment of steep green hill and then embrace the town; they have now mostly been built into houses. Our own home is beside an archway in this wall and its library is built on the thick and solid foundations of the guard-house.

As Pen is Still Remembered | 137

Until I read this delightful introduction to her mother Flora Stark's record of much later years when Mussolini broke up "for a period" Asolo's international life, I had not known that Mrs. Stark had run a silk school, Tessoria Asolana, which Mrs. John Beach established after Pen's death and the close of his lace school.

But by October 1939 "a sadness and a sort of silence had fallen on the little town." The sadness is still there though the silence is shattered.

Hélène Sullivan, now Mrs. Norman Walker, spent her early years in Asolo, and like Freya Stark whom she knows well, it was as a child that she met Pen Browning. Vivid in her memory is the fact that he talked to children as few grownups in those days did. "A child," she says, was "reasonably at ease with him." And he realized the interest awakened in them by simple things. There was the problem for instance of eating bread and butter *and* jam. "There's too much butter," said Pen, "and not enough jam. Or too much jam and not enough butter. Or there's too much jam and butter but not enough bread."

Bringing him flowers one day when he was ill, she and her sister found the bed fuller of dogs than of the patient —dachshunds on and even in it, snuggling between the sheets. They remembered too the birds: no picture of Pen is complete that leaves out the feathered, canine and horsey atmosphere perpetually enveloping him. Hélène's father feared he would be accused of exaggeration when he told of Pen driving four horses together. The "young" Cantoni is certain he had seen him driving five, an almost incredible feat in the narrow streets of Asolo. The Cantonis she remembered well, having often gone up with them to their cabin on the mountain. She said that despite the Italian names, Ginevra Biagiotti was nordic—tall, blonde and beautiful, talking Italian with a slight foreign accent. To her it sounded like Swiss—and Ginevra loved the mountains. It seems hard to work out any scheme of dates and places. The European continent, however, had been for Pen a happy hunting ground from adolescence into his thirties. But how on earth did he manage so to introduce a daughter into the Rezzonico that she appeared to be Fannie's discovery?

Pen's christening robe, exquisitely worked in broderie anglaise by some nuns in Florence, has recently come into the hands of the London Browning Society and is destined for the Casa Guidi—thus returning to the place of Pen's birth. He gave it about 1893 to William Forrester the gardener of a friend in Venice for his first-born child, wryly observing that he had no need of it. Characteristically the friendship with the gardener seems to have been as warm as with his employer. But had Pen waited for the days in Asolo, his grandchild might have worn the robe—did Pen, one wonders, while treating Ginevra as a daughter, ever openly admit the relationship?

In appearance Pen was, Hélène said, pleasanter looking than one would fancy from either Mrs. Luhan's or Michael Field's descriptions: the checks which I thought eccentric for habitual wear were very much the fashion in the Italy of that date. Though his face was red, he "looked very clean and neat for an old man to a little girl." "Dapper" was the word she would have chosen, yet the comic touch so many have spoken of is suggested by her further

As Pen is Still Remembered

comparison to Tweedledum and Tweedledee! He was in character she felt "a loner," who at a later date in the calendar and an earlier one in his own life would have been a hippie.

Asolo was a desperately poor village, of which Mrs. Bronson had been the guardian angel; and the Brownings had succeeded Mrs. Bronson. But an interesting set-up existed both there and in neighbouring villages whereby some care was taken of the poorest. On a given day—Friday in Asolo—the kitchen door was open in every better-off household and a bag of bread hung up from which a "slice" as it was called, actually more like a large muffin, was given to each man or woman asking for it. In a drawer were coins, admittedly not of high value but usually highly valued, one of which went with the bread. At request anyone was given an extra supply for relatives left at home. Hélène herself once made the distribution: what remains in her mind is sadly enough the look of hate which one old woman gave her. While it is more blessed to give than to receive, it may also be easier.

At the other extreme were skilled beggars who became well-known, living, albeit scantily, on Asolo's dole of Friday and that of neighbouring villages on Saturday, Sunday and as nearly through the week as their walking powers would take them.

It was, as Hélène remarked, a period "lovely for us, dreadful for them." The lovely included the doctors, lawyers and professional men who, in a village like Asolo, usually owned a bit of land and a house or two outside the town. These were rented in the old fashion—giving the owner half the produce of a farm or other services comprised under the phrase "droit de seigneur." This did not really refer, as so often supposed, to the right to a vassal bride's first night, although powerful enough seigneurs might take that, but to certain agreed services. Hélène was wearing a shirt most beautifully made by a neighbouring peasant, who had become almost uncannily skilled, having had to furnish three dozen—or was it six—pondered Hélène, shirts a year for her particular seigneur. The word used for the halving of the produce was in the patois of Asolo "mezza dria."

The peasants were "charming, gay and lovely natures despite much poverty," and as we walked through the village in imagination with her memories and her photographs, I saw them, I saw *it* as once it was. A girl carrying two large pails on a yoke as she left the lovely well. "Every drop of our water came to us like that." The burnished copper vessels, "all done in the river two or three times a year. There's a kind of natural pumice and they stay polished." "The kitchen fumes?" I asked. "The country people had no stoves. They cooked on a little charcoal brasier made of cement. And even the lucky ones had meat only twice a week."

One point on which Hélène was slightly sardonic and definitely amusing was the alleged devotion of the village to the memory of "their poet" to whom a street was dedicated on his centenary. It was, she said, nothing but a good source of income to the town. The owner of the house opposite La Mura where Browning had often stayed had sold several dozen pens with which *Pippa Passes* had been written. It reminded me of Edinburgh and the blood of Rizzio constantly renewed at Holyrood (in red ink) for the visitor. Tourists are a credulous lot.

My problem as to the place where any given visitor visited Pen went unsolved. It was at the Torricella that the snakes were kept, the studio where he worked was there, the beautiful garden. But to Hélène's certain knowledge he had lived at two houses in the little town itself, one with no garden but almost incredibly large, stretching about a hundred yards across the top of the piazza, while he had another earlier house *with* a garden, but this was not so good as the garden of the Torricella. To her the Torricella was clearly the centre of a cherished picture—the old Asolo.

Mrs. John Beach, now aged ninety-six, lived for twenty five years in the "house on the old castle wall which I believe the town had made, thinking to make an Asilo for children and had stopped, finding it too expensive." Pen's father used to look at this from Mrs. Bronson's loggia, "saying he would like to buy it and build it up and call it 'Pippa's Tower.' " He died on the very day of receiving the town's consent to negotiate. Pen later bought it, and house and garden were, we are told, transformed with his accustomed skill which some have called genius.

Here the Beaches lived for what, despite World War I, were "the most beautiful years of our lives." The cypresses have today crowded out much of the beauty and the house is spoilt. The old Asolo gone, its lovers refuse to seek the living among the dead. "I never want to see it again."

But here when she lived and loved it Mrs. Beach established a silk school, Tessoria Asolana. There was still in Asolo one family who did the silk weaving which suggested Pippa to Browning. Mrs. Beach noted their "bales of heavenly silk" and persuaded them to sell the stock to her and themselves take pupils.

Autumn was the great season in Asolo, and as Hélène spoke of the grape picking I saw again a vision of the child Pen—over-eating himself on grapes, reading Italian poetry to the pickers and riding on their carts.

In those later days the ride would have ended in a village-town where many of the houses were handsomely frescoed and the inhabitants however poor took pride in their heritage.

Even when poured out on minor matters, there was in Pen a spirit of enterprise, an attractive love of life. Visiting him in 1909, Dr. Armstrong of Baylor found him in possession of a machine still in an early stage of development and called an automobile. I remember the days when a twenty-mile speed limit was thought by many to be too dangerous, when horses were terrified by a carriage thus propelled, when ladies wore special, rather attractive bonnets and veils for protection against the wind.

Pen was, Dr. Armstrong said, "as charmed with it as a boy with a new toy," describing a recent trip to Florence with infectious enthusiasm. He little realized how this toy of his would become the death-dealing, peace-shattering thing that would ruin the Asolo he so loved.

Hélène remembers the day when, as the town celebrated the hundredth anniversary of his father's birth, Pen rose from his sick-bed to make the promised speech. The thing that stayed in her childhood's imagination was the crowd in the piazza. She had never seen so many people together—and we can be pretty sure that it was their own friend and benefactor more than his father in whose honour they were assembling. The speech itself meant little to her but she was struck by its fluency and the clear loud voice is still in her memory as she heard it for the last time.

I had dismissed the one little field worker, but I asked Freya Stark about the many rumours concerning Pen's illegitimate children. She shrugged her shoulders. No one, she felt, would have been surprised had Pen claimed the "droit de Seigneur" in Asolo. "Another little peasant or two more or less."

This picture was, I must admit, indignantly repudiated by both Cantoni and the former maid. But it was typical enough of an era lasting into the beginning of the present century, to make it worth noting that the obituaries show Pen not as the employer or patron, not in fact as the "seigneur," but as a man on "the friendliest of terms" with all the peasants. It was a revival of his childhood, when he would invite his music teacher to meet the old woman at the gate.

Despite Christ Church, despite London seasons, Pen was probably more completely at home with Italian peasants than with the English aristocracy. But I fancy that though he enjoyed admiration from any source, he both by nature and by choice thought far less of class than did the world he and his father had been living in. It is noteworthy that in the lists made after his death, we find Pen owning several small houses in Asolo—let out at rents so low that the tenants could buy them when his property was liquidated. His "Intendant" Cantoni had sometimes bought to his employer's advantage, but I doubt if Pen would ever himself have done so. As a child he had wanted to give as well as to own: now as a man he could—and did. But Cantoni tried to watch his interests. When I mentioned to the Engineer the debts Pen was always running up, I got the answer "Not in Asolo. My father would never have allowed it."

I was, as it turned out, exposing myself to the most pleasing accounts of Pen as I listened to the son of his former manager and to a former servant—but is not this in itself something of a tribute? Or is the saying mere cynicism that no man is a hero to his valet?

Lots of rumours can be picked up which, however singly insignificant, have made of Pen a mere figure of fun: that he let his dachshunds breed so carelessly that their offspring became of monstrous length; that he shocked his Barrett cousins by getting up so late and drinking in cafés in the morning (haven't we all done this from time to time?); that he was laughed at in old age by the girls of Asolo because incapable of accomplishing his desires. All or some of this may be truer than the still more persistent and untruthful rumour that his debts swallowed up the quite tidy sum in fact received by the sixteen Barretts who, with Fannie, were his heirs—a sum which could later have been super-multiplied had they been able to hold on to the real estate. Think of the New York Browning Society's 1970-72 campaign to purchase the Brownings' rooms at Casa Guidi for $77,000.

Pen had faults in plenty, but I am glad I saw Cantoni and the old housemaid who had lived much nearer to him than any of the gossips in Venice or elsewhere, who may also have known Fannie—indeed the cost and size of his snakes has been by and large the most persistent indictment against him. I wish I could have met poor old Sarianna, who had always upheld his father's viewpoint yet lived contentedly with the son. I wish I had seen the snakes, listened to the birds, driven behind the team of horses. The panache of the whole thing is so significantly that of the child Pen riding in his plumed hat and saying "I am one of the sights of Rome." Now he had become *the* "sight" of Asolo: Ganymede into Punchinello perhaps, yet I think he was happy in the warmth of the little town's love and admiration.

Many who have left no special record visited him there. The "K" of *The Athenaeum* obituary must surely be the Kenyon who edited Elizabeth's letters. He spoke with real delight of the welcome and hospitality he had received, noting too that Pen "did not seek society but he had a natural, unaffected simplicity and good temper which were very attractive to those who knew him: and his abilities, though shadowed by his parents, were considerable. It is not only as the breaking of a link with two great poets that his death will be regretted both in England and Italy."

The younger Cantoni remembers visits from Bindo and his brother, and from Edith herself, but most interesting is the echo, still sounding from those who lived around him, saw him daily, experienced much kindness and loved, even if too uncritically, the man who employed not only the girls but many of the men of Asolo.

For Pen's activities in the housing field had by no means ceased. As we stood in the garden of our hotel, several buildings were pointed out to us, bought, remodelled or even built by him, the hotel itself being among them. Perhaps in some cases the town's collective memory saw his hand where it did not belong: he is something of a legend in Asolo. But a great deal of it was true—and looking a little more widely one realizes that twenty farms were included in the purchase of the Torre all'Antella, adding a further picturesque touch to this little empire of our own century.

All wrong, no doubt. No man should have such power over the lives of so many others. But, in the days when the pattern was normal, to see it exercised so as to win love is heart-warming.

Pen, for the first time since childhood, was doing his own thing, uninstructed by mother or father, unhampered over finances by a wife who (naturally enough) blamed his extravagant purchases—turning the price into the dollars, which, she claimed, they orginally were. Only some of them, but I fear that on this point Pen's outlook was indeed regrettably vague. Still he had cleared one substantial debt when repaying Fannie for the work done on the Rezzonico.

Pen was already a sick man as the date of his father's birth centenary came round—he got up from bed for the celebrations but was soon back again. As he grew worse Cantoni asked whether he should summon Fannie (they had never been formally divorced), only to receive a strong and as I gathered a profane negative. Pen had pointed out to the Intendant the drawer in which his will would be found, and had spoken of money bequeathed both to the town and personally to the Cantoni family. The only document discovered—a legacy to the little field girl Carolina Betti of 15,000 lire—certainly did not qualify. Dickens has told us in *David Copperfield* the unanimous view of a group of lawyers that a man speaking often about the will he has made commonly has not yet made one at all. The Engineer Cantoni was convinced that it had been made, but destroyed, either by Edith Story who was with Pen when he died, or by Fannie, who arrived shortly afterwards. Edith could of course have no possible interest in such a destruction. An intestacy could bring her nothing; the will might well have been to her advantage.

While one certainly hesitates in ascribing the act to Fannie, it would I think be possible for her to have done it with the conviction that much of her own money as well as his had been frittered away before they separated. But the Dickens theory appears on the whole the most probable. By Italian law Fannie would now get one third of the estate, sixteen Barrett, or Barrett-related cousins, the other two thirds. And a Barrett cousin soon arrived to "liquidate" and divide the property.

For a Browning lover this liquidation spells sheer tragedy. Pen had laboured to collect his parents' relics, had purchased the home where they had lived and loved for fifteen years, where Browning had written—or conceived—his greatest poetry. For not only was *Men and Women* mainly penned, but *The Ring and The Book* was also first imagined there, as he has told us in the magnificent opening, speaking of the Old Yellow Book and of his own dreams as he stood on the terrace and listened to the singing coming up from San Felice—

> "I know not what particular praise of God
> It always came and went with June"

Strangely enough, especially since among the papers was *Sonnets from the Portuguese*, it never seems to have occurred either to Fannie or to any of these cousins to preserve a dwelling and a collection so valuable to the world of letters. Casa Guidi was the first thing sold, and all the rest followed—down to the letters, books, papers and poor Pen's pictures, all listed in perhaps the most picturesque catalogue ever conceived and put forth by the world-famous firm of Sotheby.

Pen died July 8th, 1912, and Asolo gave him a royal funeral. All the shops were shut, the flags flew at half-mast, the Mayor took part in honouring the "Cavaliere Browning"—this was the first time I had met his Italian title, which he does not seem to have used much if at all. But it was probably current coin in Asolo.

And as we talked, Hélène Walker took me finally to the simple and beautiful Antico Cimetero—the cemetery where Pen was buried.

It may be that my imagination is playing tricks, yet I cannot help thinking, or perhaps fancying, that Fanny's feelings had, as time went on, softened about the husband who in life had seemed so impossible. Now that birds and dogs were silent, Ginevra married, daily irritants absent, Fannie was really distressed at what she felt was a cruel picture of Pen presented by Michael Field. The unbiassed reader may well judge that on balance it was (apart from the odd description of his smile as a "smirk") a fair and not unsympathetic view of a complex personality. But Fannie asked the publishers for its withdrawal.

Among her papers too is a sizeable bill for the removal of Pen's body a decade later from Asolo to Florence.

His mother and his aunt Sarianna were both buried there. Rumour said that Fannie's motive for moving Pen was chiefly that his body lay in close proximity—alone on the little promontory—with the body of Eleonora Duse, the world-famous actress. Lilian Whiting told Dr. Armstrong of Baylor University that Fannie was only annoyed —quite unreasonably—by the decision of the municipal officials to shift his coffin a yard or two when enlarging the cemetery. They were, she said, much distressed when Fannie took umbrage at this. And one can see Lilian's shrug as she says, "But Fannie is Fannie."

Mrs. Beach tells, however, a different story. Since the coffin had to be moved, Fannie decided to have it placed in a plot she had herself bought in the cemetery. She sent Mr. Beach a plan, but he found another mausoleum on her plot! Fannie then decided to remove Pen's body to Florence.

By Fannie's request a cross was made—and the Beaches chose the lovely wisteria Pen had planted, woven with ivy and evergreens. Other tributes were sent of flowers purple and white. Many people in Asolo were sad, and there might have been an imposing procession as the body of their benefactor left the little town. But the men in charge, like Pharaoh's successors who "knew not Joseph," wanted no demonstration, and Pen's friends had to wait until 8.00 p.m. before the necessary authorizations arrived.

At 6.30 the next morning the body was quietly taken to Florence. It was the town of Pen's birth, yet Asolo had become the home of his heart. What was there about Asolo? The only obvious link between Pen and Duse was this nostalgic love, shared by all who have lived there. On her last tour she had written about the light at the shrine in her wall—and in her delirium she begged repeatedly that the packing be done—she must set out for home, "Asolo, Asolo, how far away you are."

Had this feeling for the home he had found so late and loved so much been Pen's final mood also, or had the religion of his childhood persisted beneath the changes and chances of life? One cannot see him haunted by the intimations of immortality always present to his mother. And it is a sad element in today's thinking that the dying should not be reminded of death. But God does not need reminding of His care for every least being—if He did, Pen's father and mother must have been beseeching Him to bring home this child of His creation whom they had loved so well and so unwisely.

APPENDICES

		Page
Appendix A	Robert Browning to Henrietta and Arabel Barrett on the birth of his son. *Courtesy of Miss Myrtle Moulton-Barrett and Col. Ronald A. Moulton-Barrett*	153
Appendix B	Elizabeth Barrett Browning to Robert Browning. *Courtesy of the Trustees of The British Museum*	154
Appendix C	Elizabeth Barrett Browning to her brother Alfred. *Courtesy of Edward R. Moulton-Barrett, Esq.*	155
Appendix D	A Word-Picture of Pen by Isa Blagden. *Courtesy of Philip Kelley*	156
Appendix E	A Note on Pen's Curls. *Courtesy of Philip Kelley*	157
Appendix F	Robert Browning to Henry George Liddell. *Courtesy of Peter N. Heydon*	158

Appendix A

Robert Browning to Henrietta and Arabel Barrett on the birth of his son, a hitherto unpublished letter.

March 13. [1849]

Dearest Henrietta & Arabel.

I am happy beyond expression to be able to assure you that Ba is going on as well as even you would wish her: Dr. H. has just left, and tells me that nothing can be better than the state of both Mother & Babe; this last little fellow grows prettier and bigger visibly. I shall get Wilson to help my inexperience and tell you all his wonderful points; she says, for instance, that she *never did see* such a delicate & beautiful skin; what would *my* opinion on that matter be worth? We have got a famous wet nurse, from the country; our first was a failure, but Ba will amuse you, I hope, with telling you herself. We are entirely satisfied with Mad: Biondi who is unremitting in her care—as, indeed, is Dr. Harding—all goes on prosperously, thanks to God for his goodness. I put you off with a shabby scrap of note, this time, but time presses really, and next letter, shall make amends. After all, "quite well" is easily said, and gives satisfaction after all. Ba particularly begs you to apprise her cousin Mrs. Reynolds of this good news; giving Ba's best love and truest hope that Mrs. R.'s good fortune may equal her own. And Ba kisses you both with the most loving of kisses . . as, if you let him, will yours ever affectionately, R.B.

I informed Miss Mitford . . can you let Mr. Kenyon know all continues well? I wrote to him also, of course.

Appendix B

Elizabeth Barrett Browning to Robert Browning, a letter on an illness of Pen (see page 12). This is the only extant letter from the poetess to her husband after they left England, following their marriage.

[Paris, February 20th, 1852]

Darling,

You had better I think bring Dr. Macarthy or somebody with you to see Baby. He has had another attack, decidedly worse in character, & though he is now asleep, yet it may return, & we ought to know what to do at once— Dont be frightened. You know I lose my head—but really it is *best* that you shd. bring some one—

Your Ba—

[Elizabeth characteristically describes the event in detail to her sister Arabel four days later, in this hitherto unpublished extract: "I have been dreadfully frightened about our child.... He had been as well as a child could be all day,—so well, that I yielded the point of calling in a doctor, which we had decided on doing the previous night ... We agreed to repeat the dose of castor oil which acted perfectly,—we put him into a warm bath at night to quiet the nervous system.... & I let Robert go at nine oclock to Miss Fetton's, quite at ease. Well—about ten the attack came on—and much worse than usual. O Arabel, he struck out violently with his arms & legs, .. rolled his eyes .. & certainly for about a quarter of a minute, did not recognize either Wilson or me.... I, who was just getting into bed, ran out of the room for Desirée, and could not find her ... So out I rushed as I was to Lady Torrens's door opposite ours, & rang violently at the bell & begged her maid who happily came, to find out Desirée & bring her directly. I sent her to Dr. Rayner who lives near us. Dr. Rayner was not to be at home for four & twenty hours. While all this happened the child recovered himself perfectly, & fell into a profound sleep ... But I could trust nothing—& so at the risk of alarming poor darling Robert, I wrote a line to him begging him to come & bring Dr. Macarthy, the physician of the embassy, who, I knew, was to be at Miss Fetton's ... Robert thought I was right in all this but really, I did it by a sort of instinct rather than reflection. He has made merry with me since, & told people that he found me in a state of distraction running about the house in my nightgown—you know I am apt to lose my head when I am frightened ... Dr. Macarthy, however, on his arrival, after listening to the whole story & looking at Baby as he lay asleep, pronounced that no child with any serious malady could sleep so,—that it was an hysterical affection which we should relieve by applying hot water or cloths to the feet, the sole danger of it being the flow of blood to the head. It might proceed, he said, from either *worms* or the *teeth* .. he would see better in the morning."]

Appendices | 155

Appendix C

Elizabeth Barrett Browning to Alfred Barrett on the loss of a trunk containing Pen's clothes (see page 9). It is addressed to Marseilles where her brother was a customs official. It is hitherto unpublished.

Lyons—Saturday night—
[23 June 1855]

My dearest Alfred,

Will you help us? We have lost a box—a square deal box with a black top—it is locked & contains, hats, collars, lace &c— "Robert Browning" is written on it somewhere. Wilson can only remember that she saw it on board the Bastia boat, "L'Industrie" from whence our things were supposed to be conveyed to the customhouse, & from thence again to the Hotel des Empereurs. Do be so kind as to make it out for us, as the loss will be considerable—three hats of Penini's in it,—& how is he to appear in Paris? If the box is recoverable, do send it in the quickest way to Robert's address, in Paris, 138 Avenue des Champs Elysées. Robert says that the address on the box is written on one side of the lid on the wood. There will also be on the box marks of its having come from Firenze to Livorno by railroad. Reward anybody who will find it, & make a note of all the expense incurred and we will pay you again of course—

Dearest Alfred, I meant to write to you from Paris, to say how I took your flowers with me & the remembrance of all your kindness to me & mine. May God bless you. So sorry I was to miss seeing you this morning—yet adieus are not the best part of love—

Penini said, "Dear mama I like your uncle so much." "But he isn't my uncle Penini, but your's! and when you see your other uncles then you'll be able to consider which you like best." "Well," said he meaningly,—*"for the present,* I like Alfred *leally* nearly as much as you & papa."

I told you you had won his heart at once, & no wonder.

In the greatest haste & with all our love,
believe me, Your ever attached Ba—

With the greatest speed, to Paris—as our stay there is so uncertain. I dare say at least ten pounds worth of things are in the box besides ms. notes to a book—

Appendix D

A word-picture of Pen by Isa Blagden, from her novel, *Agnes Tremorne* (London: Smith, Elder, and Co., 1861), II, 165. Shortly after its release, E.B.B. wrote: "I have just had a letter from Arabel in which she speaks of [your] book . . . 'The portrait she draws of Giacinto answers exactly to Penini. Of course she meant to represent him. As I read it I saw Pennini before me.' The curious thing is that though Giacinto reminded me too of Pen, I never thought you did it consciously. Thank you my Isa. That adds a flower to my nosegay of pleasure in the book."

On Monday Giacinto resumed his sittings, and at ten o'clock he was duly stationed in the studio. He had washed his face, combed out his long brown curls, and stuck a carnation in his round felt hat, which was his idea of making a toilette.

He was a very pretty boy, not so much from regularity of features as general beauty of countenance. He had a broad full forehead, on each side of which his hair fell in long thick curls, and his eyes were large and bright, and set wide apart. The dark eyelashes gave them an expression of great sweetness as well as intelligence. His mouth was well-cut, though somewhat large, and his teeth were white and even. The profile was not so good as the full face. There was a peculiarity in his features such as one sometimes sees in the faces of children not destined to live till manhood; an entire completion, as it were, of the infantine beauty. There is no room for the growth of the flower in that symmetrical and finished bud; or rather the flower itself has bloomed prematurely, and must fall from the stem. This expression always gives a peculiar interest to the face on which it is seen.

There was something precocious in every way about Giacinto. His early associations with artists, and the insensible effect of listening to their conversation and witnessing their habits, might have produced this in some respects. An extremely sensitive organization was another reason. His love for Agnes was something extraordinary in its depth and exclusiveness, and some would have smiled and some would have sighed in observing it.

Appendix E

A Note on Pen's Curls, taken from an unpublished recollection written by Henry Edward Plantagenet Cottrell (1851-1938) to his daughter, Mrs. G. K. Spruit.

Young Browning and your father were as children constantly playmates together as Mrs. Browning and your grandmother were girl friends and continued to be intimate to the time when "Penn's" [sic] mother died in Florence. She was buried in the British Cemetery just outside, at side of the Fiesole gate, her grave being very close to the grave where four of grandmother's children who died in infancy and two of her aunts were also buried. Your Father after Penn's mother died took him to the hair dresser to have his curls cut off, his own having been cut off almost a year earlier—but Mrs. Browning would not have Penns cut off while she lived, much to Penn's disgust and your father recollects how delighted Penn was at having them cut!

Appendix F

Robert Browning to Henry George Liddell, Dean of Christ Church, a hitherto unpublished letter.

19 Warwick Crescent
Upper Westbourne Terrace,
Oct. 17, '68

My dear Sir,

May I venture to beg a favour of your kindness,—so great a favour, indeed, that it may perhaps justify such a liberty on my part. Can you permit my son to matriculate at Christchurch, with as little delay as possible? I had hoped he would enter Balliol; but, at the last moment, and however reluctantly, I seem to perceive that my choice of a College has been a wrong one, and that his qualifications would serve him in better stead elsewhere. The first twelve years of his life were spent abroad,—and it could hardly be helped that his early studies were too many and too varied—of little or no immediate use in an English education, though suitable enough to the profession for which I would prepare him,—diplomacy. My own feeling for strict and complete scholarship led me at first to fancy that this might be combined with lighter acquisitions and modern languages—to a greater extent than it now appears advisable to anticipate: and unluckily this "now" comes somewhat late in the day, as my son is nineteen. He has worked for the last twelve months under the direction of Mr. Jowett (concerning my obligations to whom I will not trust myself with a poor word here). He will inform you more particularly both of what the young man may—and may not—be expected to do—and will also mention why I consider it so important a point that my son should be allowed to matriculate and reside during the present term. The request may easily exceed your ability to grant: it will not, I think, be more than your goodness can,—under the exceptional circumstances,—understand and forgive. Pray believe me,

My dear Sir,
Yours very faithfully
Robert Browning.

SELECTED BIBLIOGRAPHY

Barclay, Evelyn. *Diary.* (Baylor Browning Interests, Ser. 5.) Waco, Tex., 1932.

Beach, Mrs. John P. *Tessoria Asolando: Pippa Silks.* Asolo, Veneto, 1927.

Benét, William Rose, ed. *From Robert and Elizabeth Browning. A Further Selection of the Barrett-Browning Family Correspondence.* London, 1936.

Bronson, Katherine DeKay. "Browning in Asolo." *Century Magazine,* 59 (1900), 920-31.

————. "Browning in Venice." *Cornhill Magazine,* NS 12 (1902), 145-71.

Browning, Fannie Barrett. *Some Memories of Robert Browning.* Boston, 1928.

DeVane, W. C., and K. L. Knickerbocker, eds. *New Letters of Robert Browning.* New Haven, Conn., 1950.

Field, Michael [pseud.]. *Works and Days,* ed. T. and D. C. Sturge Moore. London, 1933.

Giartosio de Courten, M. L. "Pen, il figlio dei Browning." *English Miscellany,* 7 (1957), 125-42.

Hewlett, Dorothy. *Elizabeth Barrett Browning.* London, 1953.

Hood, T. L. *Letters of Robert Browning.* New Haven, Conn., 1933.

Huxley, Leonard, ed. *Elizabeth Barrett Browning: Letters to Her Sister, 1846-1859.* London, 1929.

James, Henry. *William Wetmore Story and His Friends.* Boston, 1903.

Kenyon, F. G., ed. *The Letters of Elizabeth Barrett Browning.* 2 vols. London, 1897.

Landis, Paul and R. E. Freeman, eds. *Letters of the Brownings to George Barrett.* Urbana, Ill., 1958.

Luhan, Mabel Dodge. *European Experiences.* New York, 1935.

McAleer, Edward C., ed. *Dearest Isa: Robert Browning's Letters to Isabella Blagden.* Austin, Tex., 1951.

———. *Learned Lady: Letters from Robert Browning to Mrs. Thomas FitzGerald, 1876-1889.* Cambridge, Mass., 1966.

Miller, Betty. "The Child of Casa Guidi." *Cornhill Magazine,* NS 163 (1949), 415-28.

———. *Robert Browning: A Portrait.* London, 1952.

Morison, Mrs. Miller. *Asolo and Its Lace-School.* Asolo, Veneto, [1912].

Phelps, William Lyon. "Robert Browning as Seen by His Son." *Century Magazine,* NS 63 (1913), 417-20.

Reese, Gertrude. "Robert Browning and His Son." *PMLA,* 61 (1946), 784-803.

Sotheby, Wilkinson, and Hodge. *The Browning Collections. Catalogue of . . . the property of R. W. Barrett Browning . . .* [London, May 1-8, 1913].

Taplin, Gardner B. *The Life of Elizabeth Barrett Browning.* New Haven, Conn., 1957.

Ward, Maisie. *Robert Browning and His World.* Vol. I: *The Private Face (1812-1861);* Vol. II: *Two Robert Brownings? (1861-1889).* New York, 1967, 1969.

Whiting, Lilian. *The Brownings: Their Life and Art.* Boston, 1911.

INDEX

Abbé (Pen's teacher), 26, 27, 30, 31, 46
Alessandro (Pen's childhood friend), 27, 35, 41-42
Alexandra, Princess of Denmark, 43
Annunciata (E.B.B.'s maid), 25-26, 28, 46
Armstrong, A. J., 116, 142, 149
Asolando, 108, 124, 126
Asolo, 60, 69, 106, 109, 122, 136-137, 139-140, 148, 149-150
   "Droit de seigneur," 139-140, 143
   Lace-making and weaving, 122-123, 124, 126, 134, 137, 141-142
   Pen's life in, 124-125, 126, 128-129, 132-133, 141, 142-143, 145-146
Asolo and the Brownings, 123n.
Aurora Leigh, 9, 24, 107, 130

Bagni di Lucca, 13, 15, 25
Balliol College, Oxford, 45, 48-49, 50, 63
Baly, Elaine, 111-112, 113, 114n.
Barclay, Evelyn, 106
Barrett, Alfred Price Moulton-, 155
Barrett, Arabella Barrett Moulton-, 6, 8, 9, 10, 12, 14, 15, 16, 21, 26, 35, 38, 153
   "Ragged Schools," 3-4, 39-41

Relationship with Browning, 39, 55
Relationship with Pen, 17, 39, 41
Barrett, Charles John Barrett Moulton-, 131
Barrett, Edward Barrett Moulton-, 10, 16, 55-56, 131-132
Barrett, George Goodin Barrett Moulton-, 16, 55, 57-58, 59
Barrett, Octavius Butler Barrett Moulton-, 58, 59
Baylor University, 6, 48, 114, 116, 142, 149
Beach, Mrs. John, 137, 141-142, 149
Belloc, Hilaire, 54
Bene, Signora del, 26
Betti, Carolina, 147
Biagiotti, Ginevra (later Cantoni), 109-111, 112, 118, 128, 133, 134, 138, 148
   Appearance, 109, 138
Biondi, Mme. (Wet-nurse), 5, 8, 13, 153
Blagden, Isa, 34-35, 37, 42, 43, 44, 46, 48, 53, 56, 57, 64
   Description of Pen, 156
Bonaparte, Napoleon, 11
Bracken, Willie, 43
Bronson, Katharine deKay, 118, 132-133, 139, 141
Brown, Mr. & Mrs. Walter F., 129

Browning, Cecil Barrett, 114
Browning, Elizabeth Barrett, 8, 9, 11, 12, 17, 25, 27, 29, 30, 31, 51, 55, 56, 58, 130, 149, 154
   Attitude to class distinction, 26
   Censorship of Pen's books, 6
   Chapel in memory of, 72, 119
   Death, 34-35, 107
   Drug addiction, 5, 33, 36
   Interest in spiritualism, 14-15, 31-32
   Letters:
     To Alfred Barrett, 155
     To her father, 10
     To her sisters, 3-4, 5, 8, 10, 11, 14, 16, 17, 21-22, 31-32, 154
     To Isa Blagden, 156
     To Robert Browning, 122, 130-131, 154
   Miscarriages, 1, 2, 4, 6
   Pen's birth, 1-2
   Political views, 32-33
   Religious views, 6, 8, 61-62
   See also specific works
Browning, Fannie Coddington, 39, 71, 106-119 *seriatim*, 121-122, 129, 130, 133, 145, 146, 147, 148
   Appearance, 112
   Breakdown of marriage, 108-113
Browning, Reuben, 111
Browning, Robert, 1, 2, 5, 8, 10, 24, 27, 33, 37, 47, 51, 61, 62, 63, 105, 111, 127, 129, 147
   Attack on FitzGerald, 106-107
   Attack on Horsley, 66
   Attitude to spiritualism, 14-15, 32
   Fellow of Balliol, 48
   Last illness and death, 106-108
   Letters, 6, 36, 42, 43, 50, 55, 57, 58, 59, 60, 62, 64, 69-70, 72, 106, 110, 153, 158
     Destruction of, 71, 131
     To E.B.B., 122, 130-131
     To Isa Blagden, 37, 42, 43, 44, 45, 46, 48, 53, 56, 57, 64
     To Mrs. FitzGerald, 67-68, 106
   Parental attitude, 64, 67, 68-69
   Pen's "agent," 64-66
   Pen's depiction of, 63, 65
   Relationship with Arabel Barrett, 39, 55
   Social life, 33, 38, 44, 106
   Social status, 53-54, 55
   View of Pen's character, 45, 46, 51, 55, 68
   See also specific works
Browning, Robert, Sr., 38, 53, 60
Browning, Robert Wiedeman Barrett
   Adolescence, 37-62
   Appearance, 9, 17, 36, 46-47, 120, 128, 130, 135, 138-139, 148, 154, 157
   Architectural ability, 105, 118-119, 129, 133, 136, 141
   Birth, 1-2
   Character, 27, 45-46, 49-50, 51, 58-59, 108, 110, 116, 117, 118, 121, 123, 127-128, 144, 145
     Generosity, 26
     Lack of self-confidence, 45, 66, 67, 68
     Loyalty, 113, 118, 119
   Childhood, 2-36
     Appearance, 9, 17, 36, 46-47
     Birthdays, 4, 12, 17, 23, 26
     Books, 6, 25
     Clothes, 8-9, 11, 29, 32, 155

Index | 163

Browning, R. W. B. *(Cont.)*
   Excitable nature, 7, 9, 11-12
   Languages, 11, 13, 21, 23-24, 31
   Pony-riding, 29, 38, 145
   Verses, 18-20, 21-22, 125-126
   Wet-nurse, 5, 8, 13, 153
   Class consciousness, 10, 26, 41-42, 54, 143
   Death and burial, 148-150
   Dislike of England, 10-11, 17, 38
   Education, 6, 15, 23-25, 27, 30-31
     In England, 42-43, 44-45, 47-51, 56-57, 63
   Estate, 144, 146, 148
     Will, 146-147
   Extravagance, 57-58, 59, 112-113, 117, 118, 144, 146
   Health, 47, 106, 119, 128, 137, 142, 146
   Illegitimate children, 59-60, 111-112, 114, 115, 138, 143
   Life in Asolo, 122-123, 124-125, 128-129, 132-133, 141, 142-143, 145-146
   Love of animals, 52, 109, 112, 117, 124-126, 137, 145
   Marriage, 72, 105-119
     Breakdown of marriage, 108-113
   Move to England, 35-36, 41
   Musical aptitude, 4, 24-25, 31, 129
   Nationality, 35, 42, 129
   Origin of nickname, 2
   Painting and sculpture, 62, 63-71, 105, 106, 111, 118, 130, 135
     Appraisal of, 63, 65-66
     Exhibitions, 64-65, 66, 67, 69, 70
     Illustrations of, 84-95
     Of his father, 63, 65
     Study in Antwerp, 63-64, 67
     See also specific works
   Political views, 30, 32
   Publication of parents' letters, 122, 130-131
   Purchase of Casa Guidi, 119, 130, 147
   Religious attitudes, 7-8, 9, 14, 15, 30, 61-62, 150
     Anti-Catholic bias, 61, 62
   Rowing, 43, 45, 48, 50-51
   Social life, 32, 43-44, 45, 48, 51-52, 52-55, 58-59
Browning, Sarah Anna, 2, 4, 35
Browning, Sarianna, 50-51, 52, 59, 60, 107, 110, 113, 117, 118, 124, 127, 128, 134, 145, 149
Browning and Shelley, 127
"Bust of Robert Browning," 94

Cantoni, Engineer, 120, 134, 135, 137-138, 143, 144, 145, 147
Cantoni, Intendant, 134, 138, 143-144, 146
Carlyle, Thomas, 11, 64, 71
Cavour, Camillo de, 34
Chambers, Dr. William Frederick, 131
Chesterton, G. K., 35, 52, 53
Christ Church College, Oxford, 50, 51, 52-53, 54, 57, 58, 143, 158
"Cobbler, The," 86
Coddington, Marie Frederika, 108, 110, 111
Cook, Altham Surtees (later Altham), 16-17, 56-57, 59
Cook, Henrietta Barrett (née Moulton-Barrett), 16, 31, 32, 55-56, 153
Corkran, Alice, 38

Cottrell, Henry E. P., 157
Cowper, Mrs., 18
Cowes, 17
"Cry of the Children," 3-4

"Delivery to the Secular Arm," 69
Dickens, Charles, 147
"Dinant on the Meuse," 92
Disraeli, Benjamin, 2
Drew, Mary (née Gladstone), 59
"Dryope," 63, 60, 90
Dumas, Alexandre, 25
Duse, Eleonora, 114, 149-150

Eckley, David, 32
Eckley, Sophia, 31-32
Estes, Dana, 110
"Eve," 123

Fechter, Charles Albert, 43
Ferdinando. See Romagnoli, Ferdinando
Field, Michael, 59, 69, 123-125, 126-129, 138, 148
FitzGerald, Edward, 107-108
FitzGerald, Mrs. Thomas, 67, 106
Flush, 3, 8
Forrester, William, 138
Furnivall, Frederick James, 60, 68

Garibaldi, Giuseppe, 34
Gillespie, G. K., 57
Ginevra. See Biagiotti, Ginevra
Girolama, 13
"Gleaner, The," 93
Gramont, Duchesse de, 32
Grey, Lady de, 43
Grove, W. H., 114, 115

Hahn, Clara, 109

Harding, Dr., 153
Hawthorne, Julian, 54
Hawthorne, Nathaniel, 46-47
Hawthorne, Sophia (née Peabody), 46
Heyermans, Jean-Arnould, 63-64
"Hope," 89, 112
Horsley, John Callcot, 66
Hosmer, Harriet, 29

Italy, Unification of, 30, 32-33, 34, 61

James, Henry, 13, 32, 105, 108, 118, 130, 132-133
Jameson, Anna Brownell, 1
Jowett, Benjamin, 45, 47-48, 49-50, 54, 60, 64, 65-66, 158

Kenyon, Sir Frederick G., 145
Kenyon, John, 17, 153
Knebworth, 43-44

Landor, Walter Savage, 26, 28, 36
Laurens, J. P., 68
Lehmann, Rudolph, 62
Liddell, Henry G., 158
Lockhead, Marion, 39n.
London, 10, 16, 36, 40, 67, 69, 72, 143
London Browning Society, 60, 138
Lucerne, 9
Luhan, Mabel Dodge, 109, 113, 115, 117, 118, 119, 120, 130, 138
Lytton, Sir Edward, 43-44

McAleer, Edward C., 67
Macarthy, Dr., 152
Marks, Jeannette, 55-56
Men and Women, 37, 147

Millais, Sir John, 59, 64, 65
  Encouragement of Pen's painting, 63
Miller, Betty, 108
Milsand, Joseph Antoine, 68-69
"Mr. Sludge The Medium," 15
Mitford, Mary Russell, 3, 153
"Moonrise, The," 85

Napoleon III, 12, 24-25, 32-33, 34
New York Browning Society, The, 144
Nightingale, Florence, 50
"Nude Study," 91

Ogle, Miss, 27
Orr, Mrs. Sutherland, 41-42
Oxford, 43, 44-45, 47-51, 53, 54, 57, 62, 130

Papal States, 32, 61
Paracelsus, 127
Paris, 9, 10, 11, 12, 16, 21, 35, 37, 61, 64, 70, 155
Parleyings with Certain People of Importance, 66
Peruzzi, Bindo, 119-120, 145
Peruzzi, Edith. *See* Story, Edith
Phelps, William Lyon, 105, 123, 129-131
Pippa Passes, 133-134, 140, 141
Pisa, 1
Pius IX, Pope, 30, 34, 61
"Pompilia," 88
"Portrait of Robert Browning," 95
Pottle, Frederick, 127
Prince of Wales, 43, 45

"Ragged Schools," 3-4, 39-41
Reid, Mayne, 25

Reynolds, Arabella, 153
Ring and The Book, The, 147
Robinson, Mary ("Minny"), 10
Rodin, Auguste, 63, 65, 68
Romagnoli, Elizabeth. *See* Wilson, Elizabeth
Romagnoli, Ferdinando, 13-14, 15, 28, 35, 41, 46, 61, 62, 70, 109, 118
Romagnoli, Orestes, 25, 28, 35
Rome, 15, 29, 30, 32, 33, 34

St. Enogat, 38
Sartoris, Adelaide Kemble, 25
Sartoris, May, 15-16
  Pen's poem for, 21-22
Sayce, A. H., 121-122
Schelling, Julia, 121, 122-123
Shaftesbury, Lord, 39-40
Sheridan, Brinsley, 17
Siena, 6, 29, 30, 33
Smith, Annie Egerton, 59
Smith, George, 64, 65, 130-131
Sonnets From The Portuguese, 148
Spiritualism, 14-15, 31-32
Stark, Freya, 105, 135-137, 143
"Still-life," 84
Story, Edith (later Countess Peruzzi), 13, 15-16, 21, 26, 30, 46, 113, 116-117, 119-120, 145, 147
Story, Joe, 13, 15
Story, William Wetmore, 13, 42, 43, 113
Stowe, Harriet Beecher, 31
Sullivan, Hélène (later Walker), 137, 138-139, 140-141, 142-143, 148

Tadema, Sir Lawrence Alma-, 69
Tennyson, Alfred Lord, 38, 71, 107-108

Texas, University of, 38
Thackeray, Anne (Lady Ritchie), 15, 38-39, 59, 113
Their First Ten Years, 39n.
Torre all'Antella, 129, 133, 146
Torricella, The, 133, 141

Venice, 7-8, 70, 114
  Palazzo Rezzonico, 72, 105-106, 108-109, 111, 117-118, 119, 121, 122, 129, 130, 135, 138, 146
Ventnor, 17
"Vespers," 84
Victor Emmanuel, King, 30, 34

Virgil, 30, 56

Westmorland, Lady, 43
Whiting, Lilian, 115-116, 117, 121, 130, 149
Wilson, Elizabeth (later Romagnoli), 1, 3, 5, 7, 8, 9, 10, 11, 12, 13, 28, 33, 35, 36, 46, 109, 118
  Marriage, 25, 61
  Psychical experiences, 14-15
  Religious mania, 28, 109
Wise, Thomas J., 71
"Woman at her Devotions," 87
Wormeley, Katherine, 110-111

About the Author

Maisie Ward was born in the Isle of Wight while Queen Victoria still spent part of each year there. Through her father, Wilfrid Ward, editor of the *Dublin Review* and a biographer of Newman, she began a personal contact with the leading writers of the day which, as co-founder with her husband of the publishing house of Sheed and Ward, she has maintained. On her mother's side she is descended from John Winthrop, the very Puritan governor of the Massachusetts Bay Colony. Her own books have been mainly biographies, notably of her grandfather's friend (and enemy) Newman, and of her own friend Chesterton. Her most recent study was a two-volume life of Robert Browning which was well received here and abroad. The present volume has been depicted as its postscript.